SUSAN W. REDDIN

DAYS GONE REMASTERED

GAME GUIDE

Complete Walkthrough, Expert Strategies, Hidden Secrets, Trophies, Tips for Mastering Combat, Exploration, and Survival in the Post-Apocalyptic World

TABLE OF CONTENT

CHAPTER 1: INTRODUCTION

1.1 OVERVIEW OF *Days Gone Remastered*

Days Gone Remastered brings the beloved post-apocalyptic world of *Days Gone* into sharper focus with enhanced graphics, improved gameplay mechanics, and refined performance. Set in the Pacific Northwest, *Days Gone* casts players into a harsh, untamed world overrun by Freakers zombie-like creatures that make survival a constant struggle. The remastered version enhances every aspect of the original game, offering a smoother, more immersive experience while staying true to its roots.

In this game, you step into the worn boots of Deacon St. John, a former outlaw biker turned drifter and bounty hunter. Deacon roams through the vast, desolate wilderness, facing off against both human enemies and the terrifying Freaker hordes. As he searches for his missing wife, Sarah, Deacon becomes entangled in a desperate fight for survival, uncovering dark secrets along the way.

The remastered edition takes full advantage of next-gen consoles' capabilities, improving the game's resolution, textures, and overall visuals. Players will experience *Days Gone*'s captivating open world in a way that is more detailed and visually stunning than ever before. Whether it's the dense forests, crumbling towns, or the chaotic encounters with Freakers, every scene is a testament to the power of the remaster. The revamped game not only looks better, but also features smoother animations, faster load times, and an even more seamless experience for the player.

One of the most significant upgrades is the enhanced audio design, adding a layer of realism that was previously only hinted at in the original release. From the shrieking calls of Freakers to the ambient sounds of the wilderness, the remastered version pulls players deeper into the world, making every corner of the environment feel alive, dangerous, and unpredictable.

Days Gone Remastered retains its deep emotional narrative and gritty gameplay, allowing players to immerse themselves in a raw, unforgiving world. It's a game about survival, grief, and the human spirit's persistence in the face of overwhelming odds. The remaster elevates the original, offering veterans of the game something fresh to enjoy while providing newcomers with an ideal entry point into the world of *Days Gone*.

Whether you're a returning fan of the franchise or a new player, *Days Gone Remastered* offers an unforgettable, heart-pounding adventure that will keep you on the edge of your seat. With its refined mechanics, stunning visuals, and unforgettable story, it's a game that continues to push the boundaries of what a post-apocalyptic experience can be.

1.2 GAME WORLD AND SETTING

The world of *Days Gone Remastered* is as vast and unforgiving as it is breathtaking. Set in a post-apocalyptic Pacific Northwest, the game's environment is a character in itself alive, brutal, and teeming with both beauty and danger. The remastered version takes this already remarkable world and refines it, adding a greater sense of depth, realism, and atmosphere that draws players into the struggle for survival like never before.

At the heart of the game is the open-world design, allowing players to explore every corner of the map at their own pace. From the dense forests of the Cascade Mountains to the abandoned towns overrun by Freakers, *Days Gone* presents a world where every area tells a story, and danger lurks in every shadow. The vast wilderness is not only visually striking but also intricately crafted, with each location offering new challenges and opportunities for those brave enough to venture out.

One of the most significant features of *Days Gone*'s setting is the dynamic weather system and day-night cycle. The environment is constantly changing, forcing players to adapt their strategies based on the time of day and weather conditions. The thick fog that rolls in at night can obscure visibility, making it harder to spot incoming threats, while rainstorms can reduce the effectiveness of ranged weapons and affect movement. These environmental factors add layers of complexity to both combat and exploration, ensuring that every outing into the wild feels unique and unpredictable.

The game's setting also emphasizes the feeling of isolation. Much of the world is abandoned, with only remnants of human civilization left behind. Ruined buildings, rusted vehicles, and forgotten landmarks are all that remain of the once-thriving communities. The lack of human life creates a sense of loneliness, punctuated by the occasional encounter with hostile humans or, more often, the ever-present Freaker hordes.

Freakers are not just a nuisance but a fundamental part of the game's world. These monstrous, zombie-like creatures are at the heart of the game's conflict. They are mindless and relentless, appearing in droves, their shrieks filling the air as they swarm towards their prey. In the remastered edition, their behaviors and interactions with the environment have been enhanced, making them even more terrifying and unpredictable. At times, the Freakers move in packs, overwhelming players with sheer numbers. At other times, they will react to the sounds of combat or the player's presence, making every encounter feel tense and exhilarating.

As Deacon St. John, players will explore these dangerous environments, finding new territories, making enemies, and uncovering hidden secrets that will help piece together the story of the world's collapse. The remastered world of *Days Gone* brings a sense of immersion through its rich environmental storytelling. Whether it's a forgotten campsite with traces of human life or the remnants of a crashed helicopter, every location is filled with lore, waiting to be discovered.

Beyond the hostile wilderness, the game's human factions also play a crucial role in shaping the world. From rival bikers gangs to the militarized enclaves, each group has its own territory and agenda, creating complex relationships that influence the course of the story. These factions, often at odds with each other, serve as a reminder that survival isn't just about fighting the Freakers it's also about navigating the fragile alliances and bitter conflicts that arise between the last remnants of humanity.

The remastered version of *Days Gone* refines this setting by adding visual details, enhancing textures, and introducing improved lighting and weather effects. The result is a more immersive, realistic experience that makes every moment in the world feel even more tangible. The game's world is designed to be explored, not just for its rich visual appeal, but for the deeper stories and dangers it holds. Every corner offers the promise of discovery, whether it's uncovering a hidden stash of supplies, finding an abandoned motorcycle, or stumbling upon a mysterious encampment.

Days Gone Remastered offers a hauntingly beautiful yet unforgiving world, where survival isn't just about avoiding danger it's about adapting, learning, and making your own way through a landscape that constantly changes and challenges you.

1.3 STORYLINE AND KEY CHARACTERS

The storyline of *Days Gone Remastered* is a poignant narrative set against the backdrop of a post-apocalyptic world, where humanity struggles to survive amidst the chaos brought on by the Freaker pandemic. At its core, *Days Gone* is a story about loss, survival, and the search for redemption. Deacon St. John, the protagonist, navigates this dangerous world while grappling with the pain of his past, particularly the loss of his wife, Sarah. As Deacon fights to survive, he is drawn deeper into a complex world filled with hostile factions, unexpected allies, and dark secrets that will reshape his journey.

The Story

The game begins two years after a global pandemic turned much of humanity into the Freakers infected, zombie-like creatures. Deacon, a former outlaw biker, is trying to survive in this hostile new world, often alone or with his closest friend, Boozer. Deacon's life was turned upside down when Sarah, his wife, was believed to have died in the chaos of the outbreak. But as Deacon navigates the dangerous landscapes of the Pacific

Northwest, he learns that Sarah may not be dead after all, and this discovery sets him off on a mission to find her.

Throughout the story, Deacon's journey is shaped by his internal struggle with grief, guilt, and the desperate need for redemption. His quest to find Sarah is intertwined with his battle to survive in a world overrun by both the Freakers and dangerous human factions. Along the way, Deacon is faced with difficult choices that force him to confront the man he was and the man he has become.

As Deacon ventures through the game's world, he encounters various factions, each with its own goals and motivations. Some are merely trying to survive, while others seek power or control over what little remains of civilization. These factions, combined with the ever-present threat of the Freakers, create a world full of conflict, danger, and opportunities for unexpected alliances.

Key Characters

The characters in *Days Gone Remastered* are integral to the emotional depth and complexity of the game. From Deacon's tragic past to his relationships with others in the post-apocalyptic world, the characters bring the story to life. Here's a look at some of the key figures:

Character	Role	Key Traits
Deacon St. John	Protagonist, Bounty Hunter	Gritty, determined, haunted by his past, skilled survivalist
Sarah Whitaker	Deacon's Wife, Deacon's Motivation to Keep Going	Compassionate, strong-willed, medical professional
Boozer	Deacon's Best Friend, Fellow Biker	Loyal, tough, struggling with his own demons
Iron Mike	Leader of the Lost Lake Camp	Wise, moral compass, committed to protecting his people
Kori	Member of the militia faction	Resourceful, fiercely loyal, practical survivor

Rikki Patil	Key ally, member of Lost Lake Camp	Brave, determined, skilled mechanic
Carlos	Leader of the Rippers (cannibalistic faction)	Sadistic, dangerous, power-hungry
The Freakers	Zombies, The primary enemy throughout the game	Relentless, terrifying, and unpredictable
Nero	A militarized faction working in the background of the apocalypse	Secretive, controlling, researching the virus outbreak

Deacon St. John: The Protagonist

Deacon St. John is a complex and flawed character, a former outlaw biker who becomes a bounty hunter in a world ravaged by the Freaker outbreak. He's a man of few words, often relying on action rather than conversation. His greatest motivation is the search for his wife, Sarah, whom he believes died when the outbreak began. As the story progresses, Deacon struggles with the emotional scars of his past, especially the guilt and grief he carries. His rough exterior hides a deep well of pain, but he remains determined to find redemption through his actions.

Sarah Whitaker: The Heart of the Story

Sarah Whitaker is Deacon's wife, a loving and compassionate woman who was a doctor before the outbreak. Her relationship with Deacon is central to the narrative, as her presumed death is the catalyst for much of his pain and subsequent actions. As Deacon's motivation to keep going, Sarah represents both the lost past and the hope for a future, and her potential survival serves as the driving force behind his quest. As the story unfolds, Sarah's role becomes more complicated as her involvement in the events following the outbreak is revealed.

Boozer: The Friend and the Struggle

Boozer is Deacon's best friend and fellow member of the Mongrels, a biker gang that existed before the world fell apart. He's fiercely loyal to Deacon, though their relationship is tested throughout the game. Boozer represents the deep bond of friendship in a world where relationships are all too easily broken. His struggle with addiction and physical injuries makes him a tragic figure, but his dedication to Deacon never wavers. His storyline adds a layer of emotional weight to the game, as Deacon often has to choose between his loyalty to Boozer and his pursuit of Sarah.

Iron Mike: The Voice of Reason

Iron Mike is the leader of the Lost Lake Camp, one of the factions that Deacon encounters. As a former leader of a militia group, Iron Mike is a veteran who believes in protecting his people at all costs. His moral compass often contrasts with Deacon's more ruthless survival instincts, making him a figure of authority and wisdom in the story. Iron Mike's calm demeanor and practical approach to leadership offer a sense of stability in an otherwise chaotic world.

Carlos and the Rippers: The Dark Faction

Carlos is the sadistic leader of the Rippers, a dangerous and cannibalistic faction that thrives on chaos and fear. They are a symbol of the darker side of humanity in the post-apocalyptic world. The Rippers are ruthless, and their practices are deeply unsettling, often marking their followers with grotesque tattoos as symbols of their devotion. Carlos' faction serves as one of the most immediate threats to Deacon and his allies throughout the game.

1.4 WHAT'S NEW IN THE REMASTERED VERSION?

Days Gone Remastered introduces a wealth of enhancements and new content, elevating the original experience for both returning players and newcomers. Developed by Bend Studio in collaboration with Climax Studios, this remastered edition leverages the PlayStation 5's advanced capabilities to deliver improved graphics, immersive gameplay, and expanded features.

Enhanced Graphics and Performance

The remastered version takes full advantage of the PS5's hardware, offering:

- **Improved Visual Fidelity:** Enhanced textures, lighting, and shadow quality provide a more realistic and immersive world.
- **Increased Foliage Draw Distance:** A greater draw distance for vegetation adds depth to the environment.
- **Breathtaking Visuals:** Enhanced graphical fidelity brings the world to life with stunning detail.
- **Performance Modes:** Players can choose between Quality Mode for higher resolution or Performance Mode for smoother frame rates.

DualSense Wireless Controller Integration

Utilizing the PS5's DualSense controller features, *Days Gone Remastered* offers:

- **Adaptive Triggers:** Feel the distinct resistance of various weapons, enhancing combat immersion.

- **Haptic Feedback:** Experience realistic sensations like the rumble of Deacon's bike engine or the grip of wheels on rugged terrain.

New Gameplay Modes

The remastered edition introduces several engaging modes:

- **Horde Assault Mode:** A survival arcade mode where players face increasingly larger hordes of Freakers, aiming for high scores and rewards.
- **Permadeath Mode:** Test your survival skills by completing the game without dying; a single mistake sends you back to the start.
- **Speedrun Mode:** Challenge yourself to complete the game as quickly as possible, competing with others for the best times.

Enhanced Photo Mode

For photography enthusiasts, the remastered version offers:

- **Time-of-Day Settings:** Adjust lighting and ambiance for the perfect shot.
- **Three-Point Lighting System:** Professionally illuminate subjects within the game.
- **New Logo Options:** Customize your photos with various branding options.

Expanded Accessibility Features

Days Gone Remastered aims to be accessible to all players, featuring:

- **High Contrast Mode:** Enhances visual elements for better readability and differentiation.
- **Game Speed Adjustments:** Modify the game's pace to suit personal preferences.
- **UI Narration:** Auditory descriptions of on-screen elements assist visually impaired players.
- **Collectible Audio Cues:** Sound indicators for nearby collectibles aid in discovery.

CHAPTER 2: GAMEPLAY MECHANICS

2.1 BASIC CONTROLS AND NAVIGATION

In *Days Gone Remastered*, mastering the controls and navigation is essential to surviving the dangerous world teeming with Freakers, hostile humans, and unforgiving landscapes. The game's expansive open world requires precise control to ensure Deacon St. John can navigate smoothly, engage in combat effectively, and explore the wilderness with ease. Below is a breakdown of the basic controls and navigation that will help you get started on your journey.

1. Movement and Camera Controls

Navigating the world of *Days Gone Remastered* requires a combination of movement and camera control. Whether you're on foot or riding your motorcycle, the controls are intuitive yet require practice to master.

Action	PS5 Controls	Xbox Controls
Move Character	Left Analog Stick	Left Analog Stick
Look Around (Camera)	Right Analog Stick	Right Analog Stick
Sprint/Run	L1 (Hold)	LB (Hold)
Walk/Slow Move	L2 (Hold)	LT (Hold)
Crouch/Stealth	Circle (Hold)	B (Hold)

- **Movement:** You'll primarily use the left analog stick to control Deacon's movement. Whether you're navigating a dense forest, climbing over obstacles, or sprinting through an open field, the movement feels fluid but can be difficult in dense areas where quick turns are necessary. Practice is key to making smooth transitions between running, walking, and crouching.
- **Camera Control:** The right analog stick is used for camera control. It's essential to keep your environment in view at all times, especially when navigating through dense areas filled with dangers. The camera can be rotated to zoom in or out, which is helpful when scouting for threats or landmarks in the distance.

2. Combat Controls

Whether you're facing off against Freakers, hostile survivors, or other factions, understanding how to engage in combat is crucial for your survival in *Days Gone Remastered*. The game offers a mix of close-quarters combat and ranged combat, and it's essential to master both to succeed.

Action	PS5 Controls	Xbox Controls
Melee Attack	R2 (Press)	RT (Press)
Ranged Attack	R2 (Hold)	RT (Hold)
Aim Down Sights (ADS)	L2 (Hold)	LT (Hold)
Quick Swap Weapon	D-Pad Left/Right	D-Pad Left/Right
Reload	Square (Press)	X (Press)

- **Melee Combat:** In close combat, you'll primarily use your fists, baseball bat, or other makeshift weapons. Press **R2** (or **RT**) to execute a quick melee attack. You can chain these attacks together for devastating combos, especially when facing smaller groups of Freakers. When encountering a stronger enemy, like a human opponent or a Horde, it's best to use a weapon with more reach, like a pipe or a bat.

- **Ranged Combat:** For ranged attacks, Deacon can use a variety of firearms, including pistols, rifles, and shotguns. Hold **R2** (or **RT**) to aim down sights and line up your shot, then release to fire. Ranged combat allows for strategic engagement, especially when facing larger groups. The key to success is to manage your ammo and take advantage of the environment for cover.

- **Melee Counter:** Timing is essential in *Days Gone Remastered*. If an enemy attacks you during close combat, a well-timed press of the **R2** (or **RT**) button can trigger a counterattack, stunning the opponent and giving you an opportunity for a follow-up strike.

3. Using the Motorcycle

The motorcycle, or "Drifter Bike," is an essential part of Deacon's survival in the wilderness. Not only does it serve as the primary mode of transportation, but it's also a tool for combat, evading enemies, and navigating through the vast world. Understanding how to handle the bike is vital for long-distance travel and escaping hostile situations.

Action	PS5 Controls	Xbox Controls
Accelerate	R2 (Hold)	RT (Hold)
Brake/Reverse	L2 (Hold)	LT (Hold)
Steer (Left/Right)	Left Analog Stick	Left Analog Stick
Boost	Circle (Hold)	B (Hold)
Jump (On Obstacles)	Square (Press)	X (Press)

- **Accelerating & Braking:** Use **R2** (or **RT**) to accelerate and **L2** (or **LT**) to brake or reverse. Learning the feel of the bike's momentum is important, especially when navigating through rough terrain or evading Freaker hordes.
- **Steering:** Steer your bike with the left analog stick. The bike feels responsive but requires careful handling in tight spaces or when turning sharply on uneven surfaces. Use the bike's momentum to your advantage when navigating hills, jumps, and obstacles.
- **Boosting:** When facing an enemy, horde, or difficult terrain, hold **Circle** (or **B**) to activate the bike's boost. This will give you a burst of speed, which can help you outrun enemies or quickly navigate across the map. However, boosting consumes fuel, so use it wisely.
- **Jumping:** Use **Square** (or **X**) to jump over obstacles. This mechanic is especially useful when you're moving at high speeds and need to clear barriers or rubble.

4. Interaction and Exploration

As you explore the world of *Days Gone Remastered*, you'll need to interact with various objects and NPCs to survive and progress. Whether it's scavenging for resources, crafting items, or talking to allies, knowing how to interact with the environment is essential.

Action	PS5 Controls	Xbox Controls
Interact (NPCs/Objects)	Square (Press)	X (Press)
Open Inventory/Map	Touchpad (Press)	View Button (Press)

Use Crafting Station	Square (Press)	X (Press)

- **Interacting with NPCs and Objects:** Press **Square** (or **X**) to interact with NPCs, objects, or machines. This includes talking to camp members, accepting missions, or scavenging supplies from abandoned cars or structures.
  Inventory and Crafting: To access your inventory and map, press the **Touchpad** (or **View Button**). Here, you can craft items, check your mission progress, and view the map. Crafting is essential for survival, as you can create everything from healing items to traps for the Freakers.
  Map Navigation: The map is crucial for exploring and planning your route. Use the inventory screen to zoom in on areas of interest and mark locations for future reference.

5. Survival Mechanics: Health, Stamina, and Resources

Surviving in *Days Gone Remastered* isn't just about fighting. It's also about managing your health, stamina, and resources. These mechanics are vital for staying alive in a world filled with dangers.

Action	PS5 Controls	Xbox Controls
Heal (Use Med Kit)	R1 (Hold)	RB (Hold)
Use Stamina (Sprint)	L1 (Hold)	LB (Hold)
Use Item (e.g., Molotov)	L1 + R1 (Press)	LB + RB (Press)

- **Health:** Your health is represented by a bar at the bottom of the screen. You can heal by using Medkits, which you can craft or find while exploring. Press **R1** (or **RB**) to heal during combat or while hiding from enemies.
- **Stamina:** Sprinting, swimming, and evading attacks all consume stamina. You'll need to manage this resource carefully, as running out of stamina can leave you vulnerable to attacks. Use **L1** (or **LB**) to sprint, but remember that stamina will deplete, so avoid over-exerting yourself in tough situations.
- **Resources:** Resources like scrap, gasoline, and medical supplies are essential for survival. Gather them during exploration, but always keep an eye on your inventory, as managing limited space is

crucial. Press **L1 + R1** (or **LB + RB**) to use quick items like molotovs or grenades during combat.

2.2 COMBAT SYSTEM OVERVIEW

The combat system in *Days Gone Remastered* is a blend of fast-paced action, tactical decision-making, and survival instincts. Whether you're fighting off a horde of Freakers, engaging in a one-on-one confrontation with a hostile human faction, or using the environment to your advantage, the game offers a variety of combat mechanics designed to keep you on your toes. This section will break down the key elements of the combat system, ensuring you understand the mechanics at play, from basic attacks to advanced combat strategies.

1. Melee Combat

Melee combat is essential in *Days Gone Remastered*, particularly when you're low on ammunition or need to conserve resources. At its core, the melee system revolves around rhythm, timing, and resourcefulness, as Deacon uses a wide variety of improvised weapons to fight off enemies. From shovels to pipes, and even his fists, Deacon can use anything he finds as a weapon.

Action	PS5 Controls	Xbox Controls
Melee Attack	R2 (Press)	RT (Press)
Strong Melee Attack	L2 + R2 (Hold + Press)	LT + RT (Hold + Press)
Melee Counter	R2 (Press at the right moment)	RT (Press at the right moment)

-
  Basic Melee Attacks: Pressing **R2** (or **RT**) allows Deacon to perform quick melee attacks. These attacks can be chained together to create combos, but they also depend on the weapon's speed and durability. For example, a crowbar will deliver a slower but more powerful strike compared to a flimsy wooden bat.
- **Strong Melee Attacks:** Hold **L2 + R2** (or **LT + RT**) to charge up and unleash a strong melee attack. These attacks are slower but deal heavy damage, making them effective against tougher enemies or when you need to clear a group of Freakers in one powerful blow.
- **Melee Counter:** The melee counter allows you to defend yourself from enemy attacks and turn the tide of battle. Press **R2** (or **RT**) at the right moment when an enemy is about to strike to perform a

counter, stunning the enemy and leaving them open for a follow-up attack.

2. Ranged Combat

Ranged combat is where *Days Gone Remastered* truly shines, offering a wide range of weapons, from pistols and shotguns to crossbows and rifles. Deacon can choose to engage from a distance, picking off enemies one by one, or he can use ranged weapons as a last resort when surrounded by Freakers or other hostile factions.

Action	PS5 Controls	Xbox Controls
Aim Down Sights (ADS)	L2 (Hold)	LT (Hold)
Shoot	R2 (Press)	RT (Press)
Quick Swap Weapon	D-Pad Left/Right	D-Pad Left/Right
Reload	Square (Press)	X (Press)

- **Aiming and Shooting:** To engage enemies from a distance, hold **L2** (or **LT**) to aim down sights, then press **R2** (or **RT**) to shoot. Depending on the weapon, shooting can be quick and responsive, or slow and deliberate, especially with heavy firearms like the sniper rifle.
- **Weapon Variety:** The game offers several types of ranged weapons, each suited to different combat scenarios. Pistols are ideal for close-range fights, while rifles and shotguns excel in mid-range combat. The crossbow provides a silent option for stealthy kills, perfect for picking off enemies without alerting nearby Freakers.
- **Reloading:** Make sure to reload your weapon at the right time to avoid being caught empty-handed during combat. Press **Square** (or **X**) to reload, but be mindful of the timing. Getting caught reloading at the wrong moment can leave you vulnerable to attack.

3. Stealth and Tactical Engagement

While brute force and firepower are essential in *Days Gone Remastered*, sometimes the best course of action is to avoid combat altogether. The game offers a stealth mechanic that allows Deacon to sneak around enemies, avoiding detection and taking out foes quietly when necessary.

Action	PS5 Controls	Xbox Controls
Crouch	Circle (Hold)	B (Hold)
Move Silently	L2 (Hold)	LT (Hold)
Throwing Weapons	L1 (Hold) + R1 (Press)	LB (Hold) + RB (Press)
Use Cover	L1 (Hold)	LB (Hold)

- **Crouching and Moving Silently:** Hold **Circle** (or **B**) to crouch and move quietly, minimizing noise and making it harder for enemies to hear your footsteps. When moving stealthily, hold **L2** (or **LT**) to stay low to the ground and avoid detection.
- **Throwing Weapons and Distractions:** Deacon can throw rocks, bottles, or other objects to distract enemies, creating an opening to sneak past or line up a stealthy takedown. To throw, hold **L1** (or **LB**) and press **R1** (or **RB**) to toss an object. The sound will draw the attention of nearby enemies, allowing you to slip by unnoticed.
- **Using Cover:** In combat, always be mindful of your surroundings. Use **L1** (or **LB**) to take cover behind walls, trees, or vehicles. From there, you can peek out and engage enemies while minimizing your exposure to gunfire or Freaker attacks.

4. Freaker Hordes and Environmental Combat

One of the most thrilling aspects of *Days Gone Remastered* is dealing with the Freaker hordes, massive swarms of the infected that can overwhelm you if you're not careful. The game's combat system incorporates horde battles as a core element, requiring you to think strategically about how to deal with these overwhelming threats.

Action	PS5 Controls	Xbox Controls
Throw Molotov Cocktail	L1 + R1 (Hold + Press)	LB + RB (Hold + Press)
Place Explosives	L1 + R2 (Hold + Press)	LB + RT (Hold + Press)
Set Traps	L2 + R1 (Hold + Press)	LT + RB (Hold + Press)

- **Molotovs and Explosives:** When faced with a horde, you can use explosive weapons to create distractions or eliminate large groups of Freakers. Press **L1 + R1** (or **LB + RB**) to throw a Molotov cocktail, or **L1 + R2** (or **LB + RT**) to place an explosive device. These weapons are devastating, but they can also attract even more Freakers if you're not careful.
- **Setting Traps:** You can also set traps to lure and kill large numbers of Freakers at once. Use **L2 + R1** (or **LT + RB**) to place traps like bear traps or explosive barrels. Position them strategically to catch Freakers off guard, creating an area of control during horde encounters.

5. Tactical Use of the Environment

In *Days Gone Remastered*, the environment is not just a backdrop for combat but a tool you can use to your advantage. Whether you're hiding behind trees, using buildings for cover, or setting up traps in choke points, the environment plays a vital role in how you approach combat.

- **Environmental Hazards:** Look out for environmental hazards like gas cans, explosive barrels, and other objects that can be used to trigger chain reactions. Shooting a gas can or hitting a barrel with a bullet can cause a powerful explosion, taking out enemies in the vicinity.
- **Ambush Points:** Some areas of the game world are designed with ambushes in mind, allowing you to pick off enemies as they pass through narrow corridors or choke points. Use the terrain to your advantage by setting up ambushes from above or from behind cover.

2.3 STEALTH MECHANICS

Stealth is an essential element of *Days Gone Remastered*, especially when facing overwhelming odds like Freaker hordes or hostile human enemies. The ability to avoid detection, silently take down enemies, and manipulate the environment to your advantage can often mean the difference between life and death. This section will walk you through the key aspects of the stealth mechanics, giving you the tools to thrive in the most dangerous corners of the game's world.

1. Moving Stealthily

One of the primary methods of avoiding detection is by moving silently. Whether you're sneaking past a group of Freakers or trying to get the drop on an enemy, mastering the art of quiet movement is crucial. The game offers several tools and methods to help you stay hidden and out of sight.

Action	PS5 Controls	Xbox Controls
Crouch	Circle (Hold)	B (Hold)
Move Silently	L2 (Hold)	LT (Hold)
Walk Stealthily	Left Analog Stick (Gently)	Left Analog Stick (Gently)

- **Crouching:** To lower your profile and make less noise, hold **Circle** (or **B**) to crouch. While crouched, you will make less noise, allowing you to move stealthily through hostile areas. This is particularly useful when approaching enemy camps, scavenging for supplies, or avoiding detection from Freakers.
- **Slow Walking:** Moving slowly is essential when sneaking past enemies. You can use the left analog stick to walk gently, reducing the sound you make. When combined with crouching, this technique allows you to move stealthily through environments, staying out of sight from both humans and Freakers.
- **Staying Low to the Ground:** Holding **L2** (or **LT**) while crouching will make Deacon move even more silently. This is essential for sneaking past large groups of enemies or when you're in close proximity to a threat. The lower you are, the less likely enemies are to hear your footsteps.

2. Using Cover to Stay Hidden

Cover is another crucial component of stealth, allowing you to hide from enemies and observe their movements without being seen. *Days Gone Remastered* makes excellent use of the environment, encouraging you to use natural and man-made objects to stay out of sight.

Action	PS5 Controls	Xbox Controls
Take Cover	L1 (Hold)	LB (Hold)
Peek from Cover	R1 (Hold)	RB (Hold)

- **Hiding Behind Cover:** Press and hold **L1** (or **LB**) to take cover behind walls, rocks, or trees. Once behind cover, you can observe enemy movements and plan your next move. This is especially useful when scouting out enemy camps or approaching a target from behind.

- **Peeking Around Cover:** Once you are in cover, use **R1** (or **RB**) to peek out and gather information without exposing yourself. This allows you to monitor enemies' patrols or wait for the perfect moment to strike or sneak by.
- **Leaning:** When you peek, you can also lean left or right around corners to avoid detection. This gives you a slight advantage when trying to spot enemies at the right angle, ensuring that you don't reveal yourself too soon.

3. Distraction and Luring Enemies

One of the most effective stealth tactics in *Days Gone Remastered* is the use of distractions. You can create noise or environmental disturbances to lure enemies away from their patrols or positions, allowing you to slip past unnoticed or take them out one by one.

Action	PS5 Controls	Xbox Controls
Throw Objects	L1 (Hold) + R1 (Press)	LB (Hold) + RB (Press)
Throw Rock/Bottle	L1 (Hold) + R1 (Press)	LB (Hold) + RB (Press)

- **Throwing Objects:** Hold **L1** (or **LB**) and press **R1** (or **RB**) to throw a rock, bottle, or any other throwable object. This creates a noise that will distract enemies, drawing them toward the sound. Use this technique to pull enemies away from your intended path or to lure them into traps.
- **Environmental Distractions:** You can also use the environment to your advantage. For example, shooting a gas canister or knocking over a pile of scrap can create a loud noise that distracts nearby enemies. Be cautious, though: if the distraction is too loud, it could attract more enemies or alert others to your presence.

4. Stealth Takedowns

Silent takedowns are a powerful tool in *Days Gone Remastered*'s stealth system. Instead of engaging in full-on combat, you can eliminate enemies quietly and efficiently, reducing the number of enemies you face in direct confrontations.

Action	PS5 Controls	Xbox Controls
Stealth Takedown (Behind)	R2 (Hold)	RT (Hold)

Stealth Takedown (Grab)	R2 (Press when close)	RT (Press when close)

- **Takedown from Behind:** When an enemy is unaware of your presence, crouch behind them and hold **R2** (or **RT**) to initiate a stealth takedown. Deacon will grab the enemy and silently eliminate them without alerting other nearby enemies. This is particularly effective for clearing out smaller groups of enemies without drawing attention.

- **Takedown on Moving Targets:** If an enemy is walking past your hiding spot, you can quickly grab them by pressing **R2** (or **RT**) when you're close. Timing is critical here; if you execute the takedown correctly, it will be a swift and silent kill, leaving no trace.

5. Enemy Awareness and Detection

Understanding how enemy awareness works is essential to mastering stealth. In *Days Gone Remastered*, enemies can detect you based on visual and auditory cues. The more noise you make, the more likely you are to be spotted.

Action	PS5 Controls	Xbox Controls
Enemy Detection Radius	N/A	N/A
Alertness/Visual Range	N/A	N/A

- **Detection Radius:** Each enemy has a detection radius that increases depending on their alertness and your actions. If you're too close to an enemy or make noise, their detection radius will expand, and they will begin to look for you. You can observe their behavior to determine when they are aware of your presence.

- **Visual and Sound Cues:** Enemies will detect you if they spot you in their line of sight. Avoid moving too quickly in their direction or stepping into their field of view. In addition to visual cues, sound plays a significant role in detection. Running, shooting, and throwing objects will all alert enemies, so it's best to remain quiet when sneaking past.

- **Escape When Spotted:** If you are detected, you'll be alerted with a sound and a visual indicator on the screen. At this point, you can either fight, flee, or take cover. If you're in a tight spot, retreating to a different location and waiting for enemies to lose interest can give you another chance to continue your stealth approach.

6. Stealth in Combat: Blending Approaches

While it's tempting to go in guns blazing, sometimes a stealthy approach is the better option. You can mix and match stealth with combat to tailor your approach to each situation. For instance, if you're caught by surprise, you might need to fight your way out. However, knowing when to drop the stealth and go on the offensive is key to surviving in the dangerous world of *Days Gone Remastered*.

2.4 EXPLORATION AND CRAFTING

Exploration and crafting are two essential pillars of survival in *Days Gone Remastered*. The vast, open world offers countless opportunities to scavenge, discover hidden locations, and gather resources that will help you stay alive in a post-apocalyptic world. As you traverse through dangerous wilderness, abandoned towns, and hostile encampments, you'll need to use your wits and resourcefulness to make the most of everything you find. This section will dive into how exploration and crafting work, and how you can use them to your advantage.

1. Exploration: Navigating the World

Exploration in *Days Gone Remastered* is not just about reaching your next objective, but immersing yourself in the world, uncovering secrets, and gathering resources necessary for survival. The game's vast world is filled with points of interest, hidden caches, and unique encounters that make exploration both rewarding and vital to your success.

Action	PS5 Controls	Xbox Controls
Open Map	Touchpad (Press)	View Button (Press)
Set Waypoint	Touchpad (Hold)	View Button (Hold)
Interact (Search)	Square (Press)	X (Press)
Zoom Map	Touchpad (Swipe)	View Button (Swipe)

- **Map Navigation:** The map in *Days Gone Remastered* serves as an essential tool for exploration. To open the map, press the **Touchpad** (or **View Button**), allowing you to see the layout of the land, including camps, mission objectives, and points of interest. You can also set waypoints by holding down the **Touchpad** (or **View Button**), which will help guide you to key locations, whether you're searching for collectibles or heading toward your next mission.

- **Finding Points of Interest:** As you explore the world, keep an eye out for hidden items and locations. These could be abandoned vehicles, hidden bunkers, or supply stashes, each containing valuable resources that will aid your survival. Some of these locations also hold optional side missions or lore, expanding the depth of the world.
- **Environmental Awareness:** Be mindful of your surroundings. Whether it's an abandoned building, a small campsite, or a dense forest, every area in *Days Gone Remastered* has its own hazards and rewards. Pay attention to audio cues and visual markers that could indicate hidden items or a dangerous encounter lurking just ahead.

2. Crafting: Creating Useful Gear

Crafting is a crucial aspect of surviving in *Days Gone Remastered*. With limited resources, you must use your crafting skills to create items that will keep you alive. Crafting allows you to make everything from health supplies to explosives, giving you the tools you need to take on hostile environments and enemies. The crafting system is tied to your exploration, as you'll need to gather raw materials during your travels to create useful items.

Crafting Materials	What They Create
Scrap	Used to repair and upgrade weapons
Nails	Crafting traps, creating Molotovs, and upgrading melee weapons
Planks	Crafting barricades, crafting weapons like a bat
Alcohol	Crafting Molotov cocktails and health kits
Rags	Crafting health kits and bandages
Gunpowder	Crafting ammunition, explosives, and other traps

- **Crafting Health and Ammo:** Health supplies like Medkits and bandages are essential for keeping Deacon alive, especially during long encounters. To craft these items, you'll need materials such as **rags** and **alcohol**. Similarly, you can craft **ammo** using gunpowder, which is found in various locations, including abandoned vehicles and enemy camps. Always ensure you have enough materials for crafting health items, as you never know when you'll be caught off-guard.

- **Crafting Explosives and Traps:** Some of the most useful items in your arsenal are the traps and explosives you can craft. Using **nails**, **alcohol**, and **gunpowder**, you can craft Molotov cocktails, pipe bombs, and even proximity mines that can deal significant damage to groups of Freakers or hostile humans. Traps like bear traps and tripwires can be used to immobilize enemies or take them by surprise.

- **Weapon Upgrades:** As you explore, you'll come across **scrap** and other materials that can be used to upgrade your weapons. Repairing and upgrading weapons is vital for taking on tougher foes. Use scrap to enhance the durability of your guns, bikes, and melee weapons, ensuring they remain effective as you progress through the game.

3. Searching for Resources

Exploring and scavenging for resources are at the core of surviving in *Days Gone Remastered*. Resources such as scrap, gasoline, and various crafting materials are scattered throughout the game world, and you'll need to be thorough in your searches to keep Deacon's supplies stocked.

Action	PS5 Controls	Xbox Controls
Search Containers	Square (Press)	X (Press)
Loot Bodies	Square (Press)	X (Press)
Loot Vehicles	Square (Press)	X (Press)

- **Looting Bodies:** After taking down enemies, loot their bodies for crafting materials, ammo, or supplies. Dead Freakers and human enemies can provide useful items that are critical for your survival. Press **Square** (or **X**) to loot bodies and containers for essential materials.

- **Looting Vehicles and Containers:** Scavenge vehicles, buildings, and other containers for materials. Look for scrap metal, ammo, and rare crafting materials that could be the key to upgrading your equipment or crafting special items. This loot system encourages you to explore every corner of the world, ensuring that you're always prepared for what's to come.

4. Upgrading and Maintaining Your Gear

As you progress through *Days Gone Remastered*, you'll need to continually upgrade your gear to survive the increasingly dangerous world. The game offers various ways to improve your weapons, motorcycle, and Deacon's own capabilities.

Action	PS5 Controls	Xbox Controls
Upgrade Weapons	Square (Press at Crafting Station)	X (Press at Crafting Station)
Upgrade Motorcycle	Square (Press at Mechanic)	X (Press at Mechanic)
Upgrade Skills	L2 (Press on Skill Tree)	LT (Press on Skill Tree)

- **Weapon Upgrades:** As you find more scrap and resources, head to a crafting station or mechanic shop to upgrade your weapons. Enhance damage, reload speed, and weapon durability to improve your combat efficiency. Upgrade components such as your firearm's barrel, stock, and sight to make each weapon more suited to your playstyle.
- **Motorcycle Upgrades:** Your Drifter Bike is essential for traveling the expansive world of *Days Gone Remastered*. Upgrade it with new parts like stronger engines, better fuel efficiency, and more storage space. These upgrades make your motorcycle more durable and help you traverse the world more efficiently.
- **Skill Upgrades:** As you complete missions and progress in the game, you'll gain experience points that can be used to unlock and upgrade Deacon's skills. The skill tree offers several branches, including combat, survival, and crafting skills. Choose the upgrades that best fit your playstyle, whether you prefer a more stealthy approach or a direct combat style.

5. Managing Inventory and Storage

In *Days Gone Remastered*, managing your inventory is critical. You can only carry a limited amount of resources, and it's essential to prioritize what you collect. You'll need to carefully balance what to keep on your person, what to leave behind, and what to craft with limited materials.

Action	PS5 Controls	Xbox Controls

Open Inventory	Touchpad (Press)	View Button (Press)
Store Items in Bike	Triangle (Press at Bike)	Y (Press at Bike)

- **Inventory Management:** The inventory screen, accessed by pressing the **Touchpad** (or **View Button**), allows you to check what you're carrying and craft or use items on the fly. Keep an eye on your inventory to make sure you're not overburdened with unnecessary items that could limit your effectiveness in combat.
- **Storage in Motorcycle:** Your motorcycle can act as your storage space. Press **Triangle** (or **Y**) to store additional items, such as excess resources or crafted materials, for later use. Be mindful of the space in your bike, as it's often your primary means of carrying larger quantities of resources.

CHAPTER 3: CHARACTER CLASSES AND ROLES

3.1 DEACON ST. JOHN: THE PROTAGONIST

Deacon St. John is the heart and soul of *Days Gone Remastered*. A complex character, Deacon's journey through the harsh post-apocalyptic world is as much about his survival as it is about his personal redemption. Once a member of a motorcycle club, the Mongrels, Deacon now drifts through the devastated Pacific Northwest, battling not only the Freakers but also the weight of his past. His story is one of loss, loyalty, and the relentless pursuit of finding his lost wife, Sarah. The deeper you get into the game, the more you'll discover about Deacon's past, his relationships, and the internal struggle that drives his every action.

As the protagonist, Deacon embodies the survivalist spirit. His journey isn't just about brute strength but about using his wit, resilience, and the skills he's acquired over the years. He's a man who thrives in the wilderness, able to adapt to any situation with a cool head and precise action. However, his hardened exterior hides an emotional core, often struggling with the grief of losing his wife and the relationships he had to leave behind.

Background and Personality:

Deacon's backstory as a former biker gives him a unique perspective on life in the post-apocalyptic world. He was once part of a tight-knit community, riding across the country with his brothers in arms, but after the outbreak of the Freaker virus, he finds himself as a lone wolf. His personality is shaped by this duality he's resourceful and tough but also vulnerable and burdened by a deep emotional pain. Deacon's journey is a quest for personal redemption, and his actions are often driven by a desire to find answers about Sarah's fate.

Skills and Attributes:

Deacon's abilities reflect his past as both a biker and a fighter. He's an expert in hand-to-hand combat, capable of taking down enemies with raw strength or precision strikes. His motorcycle is also a critical part of his skillset, enabling him to traverse vast distances and engage in vehicular combat. But Deacon's true strength lies in his adaptability. He is equally comfortable sneaking through a horde of Freakers as he is taking them head-on with weapons or explosive traps. As you progress through the game, you'll have the chance to enhance Deacon's skills, making him a more formidable force in the wilderness.

Deacon's Role in the Game:

Deacon is more than just a survivalist. His story serves as a central thread in the narrative of *Days Gone Remastered*. His personal struggles, from grief to guilt, shape his motivations, while his role as a protector and a seeker of redemption drives much of the story's progression. As players navigate Deacon through various missions, his character development plays a crucial role in how the player interacts with the world and its inhabitants. His relationship with others, particularly with Boozer and Sarah, provides depth to his role as the protagonist, allowing players to connect with him on a more personal level.

3.2 SKILL PROGRESSION AND CHARACTER ABILITIES

In *Days Gone Remastered*, Deacon's development is not just about upgrading his weapons or finding new gear; it's also about enhancing his skills and abilities. The skill progression system is central to the game, allowing players to tailor Deacon's abilities to suit their preferred playstyle. Whether you choose to focus on combat, stealth, or survival skills, the progression system offers a variety of options that give you the freedom to shape how Deacon approaches challenges in the wild.

As Deacon completes missions and survives encounters, he earns skill points that can be used to unlock new abilities or enhance existing ones. These abilities are categorized into three distinct skill trees: **Survival**, **Combat**, and **Crafting**. Each tree is designed to improve different aspects of Deacon's capabilities, allowing you to focus on specific strengths.

Survival Skills

The **Survival** tree focuses on improving Deacon's ability to survive in the unforgiving world of *Days Gone Remastered*. These skills are geared towards enhancing his ability to gather resources, maintain health, and outlast the dangers of the wilderness.

Ability	Effect
Health	Increases maximum health, allowing Deacon to survive longer in combat.
Stamina	Boosts stamina, enabling longer sprints and more sustained combat actions.

Inventory Capacity	Increases the amount of materials Deacon can carry at once.
Resourcefulness	Enhances Deacon's ability to find more valuable resources while exploring.

Key Abilities in Survival:

- **Health and Stamina Boosts:** These skills are vital for surviving long trips into the wilderness. Whether you're running from a horde of Freakers or trying to evade human enemies, maximizing stamina and health will allow you to endure the hardships of the world.
- **Resource Gathering:** With enhanced resourcefulness, you'll be able to scavenge more efficiently. This means finding rarer materials and gathering more items, which can be crucial when crafting weapons or health supplies.

Combat Skills

The **Combat** tree enhances Deacon's ability to deal with enemies, both human and Freaker. If you prefer a more aggressive approach, investing in combat skills will help you become a better fighter and provide advantages in close-quarters combat.

Ability	Effect
Melee Combat	Improves melee damage and increases combo potential.
Weapon Handling	Increases the damage and accuracy of firearms.
Stealth Takedowns	Allows Deacon to perform quicker and more silent takedowns.
Explosive Resistance	Reduces the damage taken from explosions and traps.

Key Abilities in Combat:

- **Melee and Firearms Mastery:** As Deacon advances in the Combat tree, his ability to effectively use both melee and ranged weapons improves. You'll be able to take down tougher enemies more efficiently and adapt to different combat situations.
- **Stealth and Combat Synergy:** If you prefer a more tactical, stealth-based approach, upgrading stealth takedowns allows Deacon to

silently eliminate enemies without alerting others. Combining this with explosive traps and weapons, you can clear entire camps with minimal risk.

Crafting Skills

The **Crafting** tree gives Deacon the ability to craft more advanced items, from ammunition to traps and explosives. Crafting is essential for survival in *Days Gone Remastered*, and this tree focuses on improving your ability to use the materials you find in the world effectively.

Ability	Effect
Improved Crafting	Allows Deacon to craft more advanced items using fewer resources.
Explosives Expert	Improves the effectiveness of explosives and traps.
Weapon Mods	Increases the variety and power of weapon modifications.
Field Medic	Increases the effectiveness of health kits and makes crafting faster.

Key Abilities in Crafting:

- **Weapon Mods and Traps:** Upgrading crafting skills enables Deacon to craft more potent weapons and traps. These upgrades are critical for surviving against larger groups of Freakers or more dangerous human enemies.
- **Medical and Field Enhancements:** As you progress through the crafting tree, you can improve your ability to craft health kits and other essential survival items. This will help Deacon stay in fighting shape longer, especially during lengthy excursions into hostile territory.

Customizing Your Playstyle

What sets the skill progression system in *Days Gone Remastered* apart is the ability to personalize Deacon's skills to match your preferred playstyle. Whether you focus on combat and aggressive encounters or stealth and resourcefulness, the game offers plenty of options to enhance Deacon's abilities and customize his role in the world.

- **Combat-Centric Playstyle:** Focus on upgrading combat skills if you prefer direct confrontations. Melee combat and weapon handling will be your primary areas of focus, allowing you to tear through enemies with precision and power.

- **Survival and Stealth Playstyle:** If you prefer a more methodical approach, investing in survival and stealth skills will allow you to sneak past enemies and avoid detection, while also making the most of every resource you find.
- **Balanced Approach:** For a balanced experience, you can mix and match abilities from each tree. This allows you to be versatile, adjusting to different situations as needed.

3.3 PLAYSTYLE TIPS FOR DIFFERENT APPROACHES

In *Days Gone Remastered*, there's no one-size-fits-all approach to surviving the brutal, post-apocalyptic world. The game offers a variety of ways to approach every situation, and how you play can shape your experience. Whether you prefer to confront danger head-on, use stealth to avoid detection, or take a more resourceful approach to crafting and surviving, there are several playstyles you can adopt. Here, we'll break down tips for different approaches to help you tailor Deacon's skills and strategies to your personal preference.

1. Aggressive Combat Playstyle

If you prefer a more direct, action-packed experience, focusing on combat will allow you to face challenges head-on, taking down enemies with your firearms, melee weapons, and explosives. Here's how to approach the game if you want to maximize your combat potential.

Combat Focused Tips:

- **Maximize Weapon Handling:** Invest in the Combat skill tree, particularly the **Weapon Handling** and **Melee Combat** upgrades. These will increase the damage and effectiveness of your weapons, allowing you to deal with both Freakers and human enemies with greater ease. Aim for upgraded firearms that have higher accuracy and damage, especially for tougher encounters.
- **Learn to Manage Ammo:** One of the key challenges in *Days Gone Remastered* is managing your limited resources. Even with a combat-focused build, ammunition is finite, and you must carefully ration what you have. Keep a good balance of ranged and melee weapons so you can adapt to different situations whether you need to conserve ammo or rush in with a crowbar.
- **Use Traps and Explosives:** While a combat playstyle favors direct action, don't underestimate the power of traps and explosives. Setting traps can create an effective ambush for larger groups of

enemies, while explosives like Molotovs and pipe bombs can help clear out dense areas filled with Freakers or hostile humans. Combine your firearms with these tools for maximum destruction.

- **Upgrade Health and Stamina:** Combat-focused players will often find themselves in prolonged battles, so upgrading health and stamina is crucial. Having more health ensures you can take hits while dealing damage, and stamina upgrades allow you to fight longer without tiring.

2. Stealth and Strategy Playstyle

If you prefer to avoid direct combat and use cunning and stealth to outsmart your enemies, this playstyle allows you to carefully plan your moves, take down enemies silently, and stay off the radar.

Stealth Focused Tips:

- **Master Stealth Takedowns:** Stealth takedowns are a powerful tool in this playstyle. Upgrade the **Stealth Takedown** ability in the Combat tree, allowing Deacon to eliminate enemies quietly and efficiently. You'll be able to pick off enemies one by one, minimizing the risk of alerting a horde or hostile faction.

- **Use the Environment to Your Advantage:** As you explore, keep an eye out for places to hide or areas you can use for ambushes. Always be aware of enemy patrol routes and look for opportunities to quietly eliminate threats or sneak past them undetected. Take cover behind objects and peek out to gather intel on enemy movements before making your move.

- **Distract and Lure:** Throwing objects like rocks or bottles can create distractions, drawing enemies away from their patrols. This allows you to either sneak past them or take out an isolated target. Use your environment wisely to create openings.

- **Move Slowly and Quietly:** Invest in upgrades that increase your movement speed while crouching or moving silently. Make sure to avoid running, as it will alert enemies nearby. Hold **L2** (or **LT**) to stay low to the ground, and use the **Right Stick** to carefully observe enemies and plan your approach.

- **Focus on Stealth and Healing:** Keep health supplies on hand for when you get into sticky situations, but also focus on crafting items like silenced weapons and traps to keep enemies at bay without ever alerting others to your presence.

3. Resourceful Survivor Playstyle

A resourceful playstyle focuses on scavenging, crafting, and using every resource available to survive. This playstyle is ideal for players who enjoy making the most out of limited resources and being strategic with their gear.

Resource Focused Tips:

- **Scavenge Every Opportunity:** Always be on the lookout for crafting materials, whether it's scrap, gunpowder, rags, or alcohol. These materials are the lifeblood of your survival, allowing you to craft health supplies, ammunition, and traps. Use your upgraded **Resourcefulness** skills to make the most out of your scavenges.

- **Upgrade Crafting Skills:** Focus on the **Crafting** skill tree to unlock advanced crafting abilities. The more efficiently you can craft useful items like Molotov cocktails, healing items, or makeshift weapons, the better you'll be able to handle the hostile environment. Upgrading your **Field Medic** skill can also make your health kits more effective, ensuring you can survive longer.

- **Create Traps and Explosives:** A great way to handle enemies, especially Freakers, is by setting traps. Bear traps and proximity mines are incredibly useful for taking out multiple enemies at once. Use the resources you find to create these traps, and place them in high-traffic areas or places where you can lure enemies into a kill zone.

- **Use the Motorcycle Efficiently:** Make sure to upgrade your bike's storage space and fuel efficiency. Your bike is a mobile resource hub, and making sure it's stocked with materials will help you during your travels. A well-maintained bike also lets you avoid unnecessary combat and allows for easier exploration of the vast map.

4. Balanced Playstyle: Combining All Approaches

For players who enjoy a balanced experience, combining elements from all three approaches combat, stealth, and resourcefulness can offer a diverse and dynamic gameplay experience. This playstyle provides flexibility, allowing you to adapt to different challenges depending on the situation.

Balanced Playstyle Tips:

- **Adapt to the Situation:** Keep a variety of weapons at your disposal, including both ranged and melee. Be prepared to switch between combat, stealth, and resourceful tactics based on the threat you face. If a horde is nearby, use traps and explosives; if you're in an enemy camp, rely on stealth to silently take down targets.

- **Focus on All Skill Trees:** To thrive in this playstyle, it's essential to balance upgrades from the **Survival**, **Combat**, and **Crafting** skill trees. This way, you'll be ready for any situation. You'll have the stamina to outrun enemies, the firepower to deal with tough foes, and the resourcefulness to craft powerful items on the fly.

- **Maintain Flexibility:** Don't limit yourself to one style of play. Mix and match different approaches based on your environment. Use stealth to get close to enemies, switch to combat when necessary, and always craft items that will give you an edge in battle.

3.4 UPGRADING ABILITIES AND SPECIAL SKILLS

As you progress through *Days Gone Remastered*, upgrading Deacon's abilities is crucial for facing increasingly difficult challenges. Each skill upgrade enhances his effectiveness in specific areas, whether it's combat, survival, or crafting. These upgrades not only improve your combat performance but also unlock new abilities that make Deacon a more versatile and dangerous survivor.

1. How to Earn Skill Points

To upgrade Deacon's abilities, you'll need to earn skill points. These are gained by completing missions, defeating enemies, and surviving challenges in the world. Completing specific story missions or side tasks also rewards you with skill points. Once you have enough, you can access the skill tree to unlock and enhance Deacon's abilities.

2. The Skill Trees

Deacon's abilities are divided into three main skill trees: **Survival**, **Combat**, and **Crafting**. Each tree contains different skills, ranging from increased health and stamina to enhanced combat moves and more efficient crafting.

- **Survival Tree:** This tree focuses on Deacon's ability to stay alive. It includes upgrades like increased health, stamina, and inventory space, as well as the ability to scavenge more resources and craft essential items like health kits more efficiently.
- **Combat Tree:** The Combat tree enhances Deacon's ability to fight. Upgrades include improved melee combat abilities, more powerful firearms, and faster reload times. Skills like **Stealth Takedown** and **Explosive Resistance** make him a more lethal and capable fighter.
- **Crafting Tree:** Focuses on the ability to craft more advanced items. As you upgrade, Deacon will be able to make better explosives, stronger weapons, and more durable gear, as well as heal more effectively during combat.

3. Special Skills and Perks

As you continue to upgrade Deacon's skills, you'll unlock special perks that can significantly impact how you approach the game. These perks can alter the way enemies behave, give you combat advantages, or increase the effectiveness of your crafting.

- **Special Perks in Combat:** Skills like **Tactical Focus** can slow down time, allowing you to line up headshots with pinpoint precision. **Hard Target** increases your ability to take damage, ensuring you can withstand more hits before being overwhelmed.
- **Survival Perks: Survivalist** boosts the efficiency of your stamina and health regeneration, allowing you to stay in the fight longer. **Resourceful Scavenger** increases the yield from scavenging, helping you gather more materials for crafting.
- **Crafting Mastery: Chemist** and **Engineer** perks make crafting more effective, reducing the number of materials needed for crafting and allowing you to create better, stronger traps and explosives.

4. Balancing Your Upgrades

While you can focus on one specific skill tree, it's often more advantageous to balance upgrades across all three. Deacon's journey will throw various types of enemies and challenges at you, and having a well-rounded set of skills makes him more adaptable to different situations.

By unlocking abilities that fit your personal playstyle, you can approach each challenge in *Days Gone Remastered* with a sense of control and confidence, making your survival in this brutal world all the more rewarding.

CHAPTER 4: WEAPONS AND EQUIPMENT

4.1 WEAPONS OVERVIEW: MELEE AND RANGED

In *Days Gone Remastered*, weapons are more than just tools for survival they're your lifeline in a world overrun with Freakers, hostile factions, and other dangers lurking around every corner. Whether you're swinging a crowbar at a Freaker's head or sniping human enemies from a distance, the game provides a wide variety of weapons to fit every playstyle. In this section, we'll break down the different types of weapons available, their strengths, and how to use them effectively in combat.

Melee Weapons

Melee weapons are the backbone of Deacon's arsenal when it comes to close-quarters combat. These weapons are ideal when you need to conserve ammunition or when you're swarmed by Freakers. In *Days Gone Remastered*, the diversity of melee weapons allows for varied combat tactics some deliver heavy damage but are slow, while others are faster but less powerful.

Types of Melee Weapons:

Weapon Type	Description
Bats and Clubs	Basic melee weapons that are fast and effective in small numbers of enemies.
Shovels and Axes	Stronger weapons that deal significant damage with slower swings.
Knives and Swords	Swift, quick weapons that allow for fast attacks and efficient takedowns.
Crowbars	Well-balanced in damage and speed, perfect for breaking through obstacles as well as fighting.

Melee Combat Tips:

- **Speed vs. Power:** Melee weapons vary greatly in terms of speed and damage. For quicker kills, use light weapons like knives or bats, but for tougher enemies or larger groups, choose something slower but more powerful, like an axe or a shovel. Always have a variety in your inventory to adapt to different situations.

- **Combination Attacks:** Master the art of chaining melee attacks for a quick, efficient takedown. Deacon can string together multiple attacks to deal devastating blows. Focus on timing and positioning to maximize damage while minimizing risk.

Ranged Weapons

Ranged combat allows Deacon to take on threats from a distance, keeping him safe from close-range attackers. *Days Gone Remastered* offers a wide selection of ranged weapons, including pistols, rifles, shotguns, and crossbows. Each has its advantages and disadvantages depending on the situation.

Types of Ranged Weapons:

Weapon Type	Description
Pistols	Reliable and versatile, perfect for quick combat or tight spaces.
Rifles	High damage and accuracy, best for medium to long-range engagements.
Shotguns	Devastating at close range but slow to reload, ideal for dealing with large groups.
Crossbows	Silent but deadly, great for stealth kills and conserving ammunition.
Machine Guns	Heavy firepower for sustained combat, useful against large hordes or tough foes.

Ranged Combat Tips:

- **Aiming for Weak Spots:** In many cases, shooting enemies in weak spots (like the head or limbs) will deal more damage and allow for faster kills. Take your time to line up your shots, especially with rifles or crossbows, to make the most of your ammunition.
- **Switch Between Weapons:** Ranged combat offers flexibility, so don't hesitate to swap between pistols, rifles, and shotguns based on the situation. Rifles are excellent for picking off enemies from a distance, while shotguns excel in close combat scenarios where a quick kill is necessary.

- **Silent Shots with Crossbows:** If you want to avoid alerting nearby enemies, the crossbow is an excellent choice. With its silent shots, you can eliminate individual threats without drawing attention. Crossbows are perfect for taking down isolated targets, like human enemies or stragglers.

Choosing the Right Weapon for the Situation

In *Days Gone Remastered*, no single weapon will be effective in every scenario. The key is to always have a well-rounded arsenal and to know when to use each weapon. Some enemies require precision, others demand overwhelming firepower, and some situations call for quick, silent kills.

- **Large Groups of Enemies:** When faced with hordes of Freakers or large groups of enemies, shotguns and machine guns are your best bet. Their ability to deal heavy damage in a wide area will help you clear crowds quickly. If you have to be tactical, use explosive devices like pipe bombs or Molotov cocktails to create a distraction or wipe out multiple enemies at once.

- **Stealth and Precision:** When dealing with a smaller number of enemies or attempting to remain undetected, crossbows or silenced pistols are ideal. Use these weapons to eliminate enemies silently from a distance or when sneaking into enemy camps.

- **Boss Fights and Tough Foes:** For tougher opponents, like humans in armored gear or mutated Freakers, high-powered rifles and explosives are key. A well-placed sniper shot can take out key targets from a distance, while grenades or Molotovs can help disorient or damage larger enemies.

4.2 CRAFTING AND MODIFYING WEAPONS

In *Days Gone Remastered*, your weapons aren't just limited to what you find scattered across the world. Crafting and modifying weapons is an integral part of Deacon's survival strategy. The ability to improve and customize your gear ensures that you are always prepared for whatever comes your way. Whether it's crafting ammo or modifying your weapons for better performance, understanding the crafting system will give you a significant edge.

Crafting Weapons and Ammunition

Crafting in *Days Gone Remastered* is essential for staying well-equipped in a world with limited resources. You can craft ammunition, traps, health kits, and even new melee weapons using materials found while exploring the world.

Craftable Items Include:

Item	Required Materials	Purpose
Molotov Cocktails	Alcohol, Rags, Gasoline	Area-of-effect damage to groups of enemies
Pipe Bombs	Scrap, Gunpowder, Nails	High-damage explosive for larger enemies
Crossbow Bolts	Scrap, Wood	Silent ammunition for the crossbow
Health Kits	Rags, Alcohol	Restores health
Melee Weapons	Planks, Scrap, Nails	Improvised melee weapons like clubs, bats, etc.
Ammunition	Gunpowder, Scrap, Various Metals	Craft ammo for pistols, rifles, and shotguns

Crafting Tips:

- **Always be Prepared:** Throughout the game, be sure to craft ammunition, healing items, and explosives whenever you find the necessary resources. Keep your inventory stocked to avoid being caught off guard during intense battles.
- **Use Crafting Stations:** Some areas in the game contain crafting stations where you can combine materials to craft more advanced weapons and upgrades. These stations are especially useful for creating specialized ammo or repairing broken firearms.
- **Carry Essential Craftables:** Always have a few Molotov cocktails or pipe bombs on hand for crowd control, as they can help you deal with large groups of enemies quickly.

Weapon Modifications

Weapon modifications are one of the most impactful ways to improve the performance of your gear. In *Days Gone Remastered*, weapons can be upgraded at various mechanics' stations scattered throughout the world. These mods enhance weapons by increasing damage, stability, and accuracy, or by adding new features like faster reload times or quieter shots.

Types of Modifications:

Modification Type	Effect
Barrel Modifications	Increases firing rate, accuracy, or reduces recoil.
Scope Modifications	Enhances aiming accuracy over long distances.
Stock Modifications	Improves weapon stability and reduces sway during firing.
Magazine Modifications	Increases ammo capacity for faster reloads and more firepower.

Modification Tips:

- **Focus on Stability and Damage:** For long-range combat, focus on scope and barrel modifications that enhance accuracy and damage. This is especially helpful when picking off enemies from a distance or taking on tougher targets.
- **Upgrade Your Favorite Weapons:** As you progress, invest in modifying the weapons you use most frequently. Whether it's a rifle, shotgun, or pistol, upgrading your primary weapon ensures it will remain effective throughout the game.
- **Customize for Stealth or Power:** Depending on your playstyle, you may prefer quieter, more precise weapons for stealth, or high-powered firearms for combat. Modify your weapons accordingly silencers for stealth weapons, and larger magazines or faster firing rates for combat.

Maintaining and Repairing Weapons

While weapon modifications improve your weapons' effectiveness, maintaining them is just as important. As you use your weapons, they will degrade, losing their effectiveness. Regular repairs are necessary to keep your gear in top condition.

Weapon Durability:

- As you fight and use your weapons, they'll gradually lose durability, affecting their performance. A rifle with low durability will have reduced accuracy, while a melee weapon with low durability might break after a few hits.
- Keep an eye on your weapons' condition and visit crafting stations to repair them using scrap and other materials.

4.3 EQUIPMENT AND SURVIVAL GEAR

In the dangerous and unpredictable world of *Days Gone Remastered*, your survival depends not just on your combat skills, but on the gear you carry. From the tools you use to manage resources to the equipment that keeps you alive in hostile territory, the right survival gear can be the difference between life and death. This section explores the essential equipment that Deacon can use to stay alive and navigate the harsh world around him.

1. The Drifter Bike: Your Lifeline

The Drifter Bike is Deacon's primary mode of transportation and one of the most important pieces of equipment in *Days Gone Remastered*. It's more than just a way to get around; it's a versatile tool for both combat and survival.

Key Features of the Drifter Bike:

Feature	Description
Fuel Efficiency	The bike requires fuel to run, so managing fuel is essential. Fuel can be found throughout the world or siphoned from abandoned vehicles.
Storage	Your bike serves as a mobile storage unit, where you can store extra resources and materials.
Combat	While not as powerful as other weapons, the bike can be used to ram enemies, including Freakers and hostile humans.
Upgrades	Over time, you can upgrade the bike's fuel efficiency, durability, and storage capacity, making it more adaptable to your needs.

Bike Tips:

- Always ensure you have enough fuel to reach your next destination. Run out of fuel, and you'll be stranded in the middle of dangerous territory.
- The bike's storage can be used to stash extra items that you can't carry, but remember that it's not infinite. Prioritize what you need most and be mindful of the space available.

2. The Backpack: Carrying Your Essential Gear

Deacon's backpack is where you store all of your essential gear, including health supplies, crafting materials, and ammunition. As you progress through the game, you'll need to manage your inventory carefully, prioritizing what you carry based on your current mission and survival needs.

Key Items in Your Backpack:

Item	Description
Health Kits	Essential for healing during combat or after taking damage. Crafted from rags and alcohol, they are a must-have for survival.
Ammunition	You can carry a limited amount of ammo for your guns, so be sure to always have enough for when you need it most.
Crafting Materials	Includes scrap, gunpowder, alcohol, nails, and more. These materials are used for crafting items like Molotov cocktails, traps, and weapons.
Traps and Explosives	Use these to create distractions or eliminate large groups of enemies. Items like bear traps, proximity mines, and pipe bombs are vital in combat.

Inventory Management Tips:

- Always check your backpack before heading into a dangerous area. Make sure you have enough health kits, ammunition, and crafting materials for unexpected encounters.
- Consider leaving less-essential items in your bike's storage to make room for more valuable gear, especially if you're preparing for a tough mission or a horde encounter.

3. Health and Stamina Boosters

Your survival in *Days Gone Remastered* heavily relies on maintaining your health and stamina. Fortunately, there are several items in the game that can boost your health and stamina, allowing you to recover faster or fight longer.

Health-Boosting Gear:

Item	Description
Medkits	Crafted from rags and alcohol, medkits are your primary means of healing. Carry a few at all times.

Bandages	These can be used to patch up wounds during combat, though they are less effective than medkits.
Field Medic Upgrade	This skill enhances your health kit's effectiveness, allowing them to heal more damage.

Stamina-Boosting Gear:

Item	Description
Stamina Cocktail	A crafted item that boosts your stamina for a short period, allowing you to sprint longer distances or engage in prolonged combat.
Stamina Upgrades	These upgrades are found in the Survival skill tree and will increase your stamina capacity, allowing for longer sprints and faster recovery.

Tips for Health and Stamina:

- Always have at least one medkit in your backpack and one or two stamina boosters on your bike. You never know when you'll need to outrun a horde or heal up in the middle of a firefight.
- Invest in stamina upgrades to make your survival easier, especially during long runs or horde encounters.

4. Special Equipment for Stealth and Combat

In addition to the basic survival gear, there are several special pieces of equipment that can help you stay stealthy or give you the edge in combat. These items are crucial for specific playstyles, like avoiding direct confrontations or taking out enemies quietly.

Stealth Gear:

Item	Description
Crossbow	A silent ranged weapon, perfect for picking off enemies without alerting others. Crossbow bolts are reusable, making it a cost-effective weapon for stealth-based players.

Throwing Rocks and Bottles	These can be used to distract enemies, drawing them away from their positions or luring them into traps.

Combat Gear:

Item	Description
Molotov Cocktails	Used to create large explosions of fire that damage and disorient enemies in wide areas.
Pipe Bombs	Explosive devices that deal significant damage to enemies and can be used to clear out groups of Freakers or human enemies.
Bear Traps	Set these traps in enemy paths to immobilize or kill enemies. Highly effective when used in conjunction with stealth.

Combat and Stealth Tips:

- If you're using a stealth approach, always carry a crossbow or silenced pistol to eliminate enemies without being detected. Make use of distractions and stealth takedowns whenever possible.
- For combat-heavy playstyles, Molotov cocktails and pipe bombs are lifesavers. Save these items for difficult battles, such as confronting hordes or large groups of enemies.

4.4 BEST LOADOUTS FOR DIFFERENT PLAYSTYLES

Every player has their preferred way of dealing with threats in *Days Gone Remastered*. Whether you like to rush into battle guns blazing, pick off enemies one by one from a distance, or sneak past dangers without ever being seen, the game offers a variety of loadouts to suit different playstyles. Below, we'll outline the best loadouts for different approaches to combat, so you can tailor your gear to suit your preferred method of survival.

1. Aggressive Combat Loadout

For players who want to take on the world headfirst, the aggressive combat loadout maximizes offensive capabilities and durability. You'll be able to deal significant damage while maintaining mobility and firepower.

Recommended Gear:

Item	Why it Works
Shotgun	High damage output at close range, perfect for clearing large groups of enemies.
Assault Rifle	A well-rounded weapon that offers rapid fire and accuracy for mid-range combat.
Molotov Cocktails	Effective for crowd control and clearing out swarms of Freakers.
Medkits	To ensure you stay alive during long, drawn-out fights.
Stamina Cocktail	Useful when you need to sprint away from danger or keep up with combat.

Combat Tips:
- Focus on using shotguns in close quarters to clear enemies quickly, then switch to your assault rifle for ranged attacks.
- Molotov cocktails will be your go-to for dealing with groups of Freakers, allowing you to handle swarms more efficiently.

2. Stealth Loadout

For players who prefer a quieter, more strategic approach, the stealth loadout is the way to go. With silent weapons and distraction tools, you can avoid detection and take out enemies one by one without ever being noticed.

Recommended Gear:

Item	Why it Works
Crossbow	Silent and deadly, perfect for eliminating enemies from a distance without alerting others.
Silenced Pistol	Offers precision while maintaining stealth, perfect for dealing with humans quietly.

Throwing Rocks/Bottles	Essential for distracting enemies and luring them into traps or away from their patrols.
Bear Traps	Useful for setting up ambushes, allowing you to capture or kill enemies silently.
Medkits	For quick healing when you're discovered or in need of a break.

Stealth Tips:

- Use the crossbow or silenced pistol for silent eliminations. Aim for headshots to reduce the time it takes to take down enemies.
- Throw rocks and bottles to create distractions, leading enemies into traps or pulling them away from their patrols so you can sneak by undetected.

3. Resourceful Survivor Loadout

For players who prefer to be prepared for anything, the resourceful survivor loadout focuses on adaptability and maximizing resources. This loadout ensures that you can handle both combat and stealth situations without running out of supplies.

Recommended Gear:

Item	Why it Works
Assault Rifle	Versatile, perfect for both mid-range combat and dealing with human enemies.
Molotov Cocktails	For dealing with Freaker swarms or creating distractions.
Pipe Bombs	High damage, great for taking on tough enemies or clearing out large areas.
Medkits and Stamina Boosters	Keep your health up and stamina at full capacity during long explorations.

Bear Traps	Set traps to immobilize enemies or create a safe path through dangerous areas.

Survival Tips:

- With this loadout, always be prepared for any scenario whether you're taking down a tough enemy, sneaking past a horde, or dealing with a large group of Freakers.
- Use your Molotovs and pipe bombs strategically to control the battlefield when you can't avoid combat. Set traps in high-traffic areas to catch enemies off guard.

CHAPTER 5: STRATEGIES AND TIPS

5.1 SURVIVING THE FREAKERS: BEST TACTICS

In *Days Gone Remastered*, Freakers are more than just enemies they're a relentless force that can overwhelm you if you're not careful. Whether you're facing a few stragglers or a full-blown horde, learning the best tactics for surviving these creatures is essential for your success. This section will walk you through the most effective ways to deal with Freakers, from avoiding large groups to fighting them head-on.

1. Avoidance: The Stealth Approach

One of the best ways to survive against Freakers is to avoid them altogether. Freakers are drawn to noise, so making stealth a priority will help you bypass large groups without putting yourself at risk. By sneaking past enemies, you can avoid unnecessary confrontations and conserve your resources for when you need them most.

Key Stealth Tactics:

- **Crouch and Move Slowly:** Use **Circle** (or **B**) to crouch and move slowly. Hold **L2** (or **LT**) to stay low to the ground and reduce your noise level. This will help you slip past groups without being detected.

- **Distract with Throwables:** Throwing rocks, bottles, or other objects is a great way to lure Freakers away from your path. Use **L1** (or **LB**) to hold an object and **R1** (or **RB**) to throw it. The noise will attract Freakers, allowing you to slip by unnoticed.

- **Use the Environment:** When possible, hide behind large objects like rocks or abandoned vehicles. Stay behind cover and wait for the Freakers to pass by. Pay attention to their patrol patterns to time your movements.

When to Avoid Combat:

- If you're low on resources like ammunition or health kits, or if you're exploring unfamiliar areas, it's best to avoid combat. Instead, focus on gathering supplies and scouting out safe routes.

- If you encounter a large group or a horde, running and hiding is often your best option. It's better to live to fight another day than to waste precious resources fighting a losing battle.

2. Fighting the Freakers: Know Your Enemy

When it's unavoidable, you'll need to fight the Freakers. They're fast, aggressive, and relentless, but with the right tactics, you can take them down without wasting too much ammo or risking your life. The key to fighting

Freakers is to understand their behavior and use the environment to your advantage.

Key Combat Tips:

- **Headshots Are Key:** Freakers may appear to be slow and mindless, but their numbers can quickly overwhelm you. Aim for headshots whenever possible. This not only eliminates them quickly but also conserves ammunition.

- **Use Melee Weapons Wisely:** Melee weapons are great for conserving ammo, but they require close-range combat, which can be dangerous. Keep a strong melee weapon on hand for when you're surrounded, but be ready to switch to a ranged weapon if things get too chaotic.

- **Keep Moving:** Freakers are unpredictable, and they tend to swarm. Always be on the move, especially when facing a group of them. Backpedal while firing, and use obstacles to block their line of sight to give yourself time to regroup.

- **Molotovs and Explosives:** Molotov cocktails, pipe bombs, and other explosives are incredibly effective against large groups of Freakers. Throw them into a horde to clear multiple enemies at once. Keep an eye on your surroundings, though if you're too close, the blast radius can hurt you as well.

3. Dealing with Freaker Hordes: Patience and Precision

Freaker hordes are a different beast entirely. These massive groups can be overwhelming, but with the right approach, they can be taken down without too much trouble. The key to surviving a horde encounter is to stay calm, manage your resources, and use the environment effectively.

How to Tackle a Horde:

- **Plan Your Escape Routes:** Before you engage a horde, always ensure you know your escape routes. Look for places to take cover or escape if the situation turns south. It's important to have a backup plan in case things go wrong.

- **Use Fire and Traps:** Fire is a great way to clear out large groups of Freakers. Molotov cocktails and other incendiary devices can set the horde on fire, causing them to burn down while you stay at a safe distance. Use **L1 + R1** (or **LB + RB**) to throw Molotovs, and aim for clusters of Freakers.

- **Lure Them Into Traps:** If you can, set up bear traps or proximity mines around the area where the horde is located. Lure the Freakers into these traps using noise or distractions, then watch as they get caught and explode. This can significantly reduce the number of Freakers you have to fight directly.

- **Conserve Ammo:** Fighting a horde requires ammunition, but don't waste it on small, scattered groups. Focus on using explosive items and melee weapons for smaller clusters of Freakers, saving your ammunition for the final showdown.

4. Tactical Use of the Environment

The world of *Days Gone Remastered* is filled with environmental hazards that you can use to your advantage. From gas canisters to explosive barrels, you can create deadly traps to thin out the ranks of a horde or kill individual Freakers quietly.

Useful Environmental Hazards:

- **Explosive Barrels:** Shoot explosive barrels to create a massive blast that damages Freakers in the vicinity. These can be found throughout the world, and using them effectively can decimate a group of enemies in one shot.
- **Gas Cans:** Similar to explosive barrels, gas cans can be shot to create explosions. They are highly effective in close-quarters or when surrounded by Freakers.
- **Ambush Spots:** Look for high ground or structures where you can ambush enemies. By positioning yourself above or behind obstacles, you can shoot down on approaching Freakers or groups of enemies.

5.2 COMBAT TIPS: HOW TO DEFEAT HORDES

Freaker hordes are one of the most intense challenges in *Days Gone Remastered*. These massive groups of infected creatures can be daunting, but with the right strategy and preparation, you can wipe them out without losing everything. In this section, we'll cover specific combat tips for handling hordes and ensuring your survival when the odds are stacked against you.

1. Preparation is Key: Gather Resources

Before tackling a horde, it's important to gather resources and plan your strategy. Unlike regular Freaker encounters, hordes are far more difficult to handle, and you'll need everything you can get your hands on.

Essential Resources to Gather:

- **Ammunition:** Always ensure you have enough ammo for your guns, especially rifles and shotguns. These weapons are your primary means of dealing with large groups of Freakers.

- **Explosives:** Stock up on Molotov cocktails, pipe bombs, and mines. These will be your best friends when dealing with a horde, as they can clear large groups quickly.
- **Health Kits and Stamina Boosters:** If you get swarmed, you'll need to heal quickly. Always carry medkits and stamina boosters to ensure you can keep fighting or escape when necessary.

Preparation Tips:
- **Set Traps:** Before engaging a horde, use the environment to your advantage. Set bear traps or mines in chokepoints where the Freakers are likely to walk. This will help whittle down their numbers before you even start fighting.
- **Fuel Up Your Bike:** Make sure your bike is fueled up and ready to go. If things go south, you'll want to be able to make a quick escape.

2. Fight Smart, Not Hard

When dealing with a horde, the key is not to rush in and fight recklessly. Instead, use your environment and tactics to take out as many Freakers as possible without putting yourself in harm's way.

Combat Tips for Fighting a Horde:
- **Pick Off Small Groups:** Don't try to fight the entire horde at once. Instead, focus on picking off smaller groups as they separate from the main cluster. Use your rifle or shotgun to take out Freakers from a distance.
- **Use Fire to Thin the Herd:** Molotov cocktails and fire are incredibly effective against large groups. When a horde is clustered together, throwing a Molotov cocktail into the middle can decimate dozens of Freakers in seconds.
- **Use Your Bike to Distract:** Drive your bike through or around the horde to draw their attention. Once they're focused on the bike, you can use the distraction to take them out from a safe distance.

3. Stay Mobile and Keep Moving

Fighting a horde is all about staying one step ahead of the Freakers. They move fast and can quickly overwhelm you if you stand still for too long. Keep moving, use your surroundings for cover, and always be aware of your escape routes.

Mobility Tips:
- **Keep Backpedaling:** Use the environment to maintain distance between you and the horde. Move backward while shooting to avoid being swarmed.

- **Escape When Necessary:** If you're in danger of being overwhelmed, don't hesitate to retreat. Your bike is the perfect way to escape from a horde quickly, and you can always regroup to fight again later.

4. Know When to Call for Help

If you're struggling to fight a horde on your own, remember that you can always call for help. Throughout the game, you'll encounter NPCs who are willing to assist you in taking down larger threats. While you may not always have allies nearby, don't hesitate to reach out for support when you can.

5.3 RESOURCE MANAGEMENT: TIPS FOR CRAFTING AND SCAVENGING

In *Days Gone Remastered*, resource management plays a pivotal role in ensuring your survival. The world is filled with limited supplies, and how you manage them will determine how long you last in the harsh, post-apocalyptic environment. From gathering scrap and gasoline to crafting weapons and health kits, smart resource management is essential for thriving in this dangerous world. This section will guide you through the best practices for crafting, scavenging, and managing your resources effectively.

1. Scavenging Essentials: Prioritize What You Need

Scavenging is a key aspect of survival in *Days Gone Remastered*. The more efficiently you scavenge, the better prepared you'll be to handle whatever the world throws at you. However, with limited backpack space and fuel for your bike, it's essential to prioritize the right resources. Here are the most important items to focus on when scavenging.

Key Resources to Scavenge:

Resource	Use
Scrap	Essential for repairing weapons and upgrading your gear.
Gasoline	Required to fuel your bike, which is crucial for travel and escaping danger.
Gunpowder	Used to craft ammunition, especially for your firearms.
Alcohol	Used for crafting Molotovs and healing items like health kits.

Rags	Vital for crafting health kits and bandages.
Nails	Needed for crafting explosive devices like Molotov cocktails and traps.

Scavenging Tips:

- **Visit Abandoned Locations:** Always check abandoned cars, vehicles, and camps for essential supplies. These areas often contain scrap, gasoline, and other materials that are hard to come by.
- **Loot Bodies and Enemies:** After a fight, don't forget to loot fallen enemies. They can provide you with valuable ammo, crafting materials, and occasionally high-end gear.
- **Stay Vigilant for Hidden Stashes:** Look out for hidden caches or supply crates while exploring. Some of these are buried or tucked away in hard-to-reach spots, but they can hold significant amounts of ammo, crafting materials, or medical supplies.

2. Crafting: Maximize What You Find

Crafting is one of the most rewarding mechanics in *Days Gone Remastered*. With the right materials, you can craft everything from healing kits to explosive devices that can help you clear groups of enemies or set traps. The key to efficient crafting is knowing what to create based on your current needs.

Key Crafting Items to Focus On:

Craftable Item	Required Materials	Purpose
Molotov Cocktails	Alcohol, Rags, Gasoline	For explosive area damage against enemies
Pipe Bombs	Scrap, Gunpowder, Nails	High-damage explosive device to clear crowds
Health Kits	Rags, Alcohol	Restores health in critical situations
Crossbow Bolts	Scrap, Wood	Silent ammunition for stealthy takedowns

Bear Traps	Scrap, Nails	Set traps for immobilizing or killing enemies
Stamina Cocktail	Herbs, Rags, Water	Boosts stamina temporarily for combat or fleeing

Crafting Tips:

- **Craft on the Go:** Always craft health kits, Molotov cocktails, and ammunition when you find the necessary materials. Don't wait for a critical moment to realize you've run out of essential items.
- **Specialized Crafting:** If you're preparing for a major fight, focus on crafting explosives and traps. If you're heading into an area with fewer enemies, craft health kits and stamina boosters to prepare for any surprise encounters.
- **Manage Crafting Materials:** With limited space and resources, always evaluate what you need most before crafting. Don't craft ammo or explosives if you're low on health supplies.

3. Efficient Inventory Management: Carry What Matters

With limited space in your backpack, it's essential to be strategic about what you carry. Knowing when to drop certain items for more crucial ones is vital for surviving longer expeditions. Carefully manage your inventory to keep the items that will serve you best.

Inventory Management Tips:

- **Keep Multiple Weapon Types:** Make sure to have a mix of weapons. Carry a powerful ranged weapon (like a rifle or shotgun) and a fast melee weapon (like a bat or crowbar). This ensures that you're ready for both stealth and combat situations.
- **Leave Non-Essential Items in Storage:** Store extra resources like fuel or spare ammunition in your bike's storage. This allows you to take only what's essential in your backpack for each mission.
- **Crafting Stations:** Take advantage of crafting stations to craft large quantities of items when you have the time. These stations are useful for combining materials into more advanced gear and can help you avoid running low on important items.

5.4 STEALTH AND AVOIDING COMBAT: WHEN TO FIGHT, WHEN TO FLEE

While combat is often inevitable in *Days Gone Remastered*, avoiding unnecessary confrontations is sometimes the best option. Whether you're low on resources, facing a larger group of enemies, or simply trying to conserve your energy, knowing when to fight and when to flee is essential. This section will help you master stealth and avoidance tactics, allowing you to navigate the world more strategically.

1. Stealth Tips: Sneak Past Your Enemies

Stealth is a key tool in *Days Gone Remastered*. Many players prefer to avoid combat entirely by sneaking past enemies or picking them off quietly one by one. The game gives you a variety of tools to remain hidden and make your way through dangerous zones without alerting every enemy in sight.

Stealth Tips:

- **Move Slowly and Crouch:** Always crouch and move slowly when sneaking around enemies. Use **L2** (or **LT**) to crouch and reduce noise. The slower you move, the harder it will be for enemies to detect you.

- **Use the Environment for Cover:** Hide behind rocks, trees, or buildings to remain out of sight. Pay attention to enemy patrol patterns and wait for the right moment to move.

- **Distract with Objects:** Use rocks, bottles, or other throwables to create distractions and lure enemies away from your path. This allows you to sneak by unnoticed or set up a stealthy takedown.

- **Focus on Silent Weapons:** Use the crossbow or silenced pistols for eliminating enemies without making a sound. This allows you to take out stragglers or isolated enemies without alerting others.

2. When to Fight: Engaging in Combat

Despite your best efforts, there will be times when you need to engage in combat. When that happens, having the right strategy can make all the difference. Don't fight recklessly assess the situation and decide whether combat is your best option.

Combat Tips:

- **Take Advantage of Enemy Weaknesses:** When engaging in combat, aim for weak spots such as the head or legs. This will not only deal more damage but can also help you take enemies down faster.

- **Use the Terrain:** Fight in areas that give you an advantage. Use high ground for better visibility and cover, or retreat to areas with choke points that limit how many enemies can approach you at once.

- **Save Ammo for Bigger Fights:** Don't waste precious ammunition on smaller enemies when you can easily dispatch them with melee combat. Use ranged weapons for tougher foes or when you're forced to deal with large numbers.

3. When to Flee: Running from Danger

Sometimes, the best course of action is to simply escape. Whether you're up against an overwhelming number of Freakers, facing an armed group of enemies, or simply don't have the resources to fight, running can often save your life. In *Days Gone Remastered*, being able to recognize when to flee is as important as knowing how to fight.

Escape Tips:

- **Know Your Exit Routes:** Always be aware of your surroundings and the quickest escape routes. If you're in a situation where you can't win the fight, use your bike to quickly get away or find a place to hide until the enemies lose interest.

- **Use the Bike to Evade:** The Drifter Bike is an excellent tool for escaping danger. Use the **boost** to speed away from enemies or Freakers. The bike's speed allows you to get out of tough situations fast.

- **Don't Engage If You're Low on Resources:** If you're low on ammo, health kits, or stamina, it's often smarter to flee than to fight. Seek out safe zones, gather more supplies, and return to fight later when you're better prepared.

4. Use Distraction and Traps to Escape or Win

If you find yourself surrounded by enemies and running is the only option, use distractions to help make your escape. Throwing Molotov cocktails, setting traps, or even leading enemies into explosive barrels can create a diversion and buy you enough time to flee.

Escape and Combat Tips:

- **Molotovs and Explosives:** Use these items to create chaos in enemy lines, drawing attention away from you or destroying large groups of enemies.

- **Bear Traps:** Set traps at chokepoints or in areas where enemies are likely to pass. This can slow them down and give you time to escape or strategize.

CHAPTER 6: WALKTHROUGHS FOR MISSIONS AND LEVELS

6.1 MISSION 1: THE BEGINNING OF SURVIVAL

The first mission in *Days Gone Remastered* sets the stage for everything that follows, introducing players to the brutal post-apocalyptic world Deacon St. John must navigate. "The Beginning of Survival" is an important mission, as it not only introduces key gameplay mechanics but also provides a solid foundation for understanding how to survive in this harsh environment. In this chapter, we'll guide you step-by-step through the mission, offering tips, strategies, and insights into how to complete it successfully while setting you up for the rest of the game.

Mission Overview:

Mission Name: The Beginning of Survival
Location: Deacon's Camp / Forested Area
Objective: Complete your first objective of surviving by navigating the wilderness, finding supplies, and fending off threats.

As the mission begins, you'll be thrust into a survival situation. Deacon, with his instincts and skills as a former biker and survivalist, will need to adapt quickly to the new world order. The game opens with a brief cutscene introducing Deacon's story, his wife Sarah, and his emotional drive to survive in a world dominated by the Freaker outbreak. This mission serves as both a tutorial and an introduction to the harsh realities of the world Deacon now inhabits.

Mission Breakdown:

1. The Introduction: Learning the Ropes

The mission starts with Deacon on the move, searching for his wife after the outbreak. The first part of the mission is all about introducing you to the basics of survival in the world of *Days Gone Remastered*.

What You'll Learn:

- **Basic Movement Controls:** You'll be guided through movement and basic camera controls. Follow Deacon's movements as he makes his way through the environment.
- **Interact with Objects:** You'll interact with various objects to gather supplies. Be sure to explore every corner for scrap, gasoline, and other resources that will be crucial later on.
- **First Combat Encounter:** Your first real combat situation will occur shortly after you leave the starting camp. You'll be introduced to Freakers, the infected enemies that roam the land. Use melee

combat (L2 + R2 or LT + RT) for quick takedowns to conserve ammunition, especially since your resources are limited early on.

2. Searching for Supplies: Essential Gathering

As you continue the mission, the importance of scavenging will become apparent. Deacon needs supplies to survive ammo, fuel, and health kits are critical in this early part of the game.

Objective: Find Supplies

You'll need to explore your surroundings to gather the following items:

- **Scrap** (for repairs and upgrades)
- **Gunpowder** (for crafting ammunition)
- **Alcohol** (used to craft health kits and Molotov cocktails)

Tips for Scavenging:

- **Take Your Time:** Don't rush through the areas. Take your time to explore abandoned buildings, vehicles, and other nooks where supplies can be hidden.
- **Check Every Vehicle:** Vehicles are great sources of fuel, which you'll need for your bike. Always siphon fuel from abandoned cars and trucks when you can.
- **Be Careful in Open Areas:** In this early part of the game, Freakers will appear more frequently in the open, especially in larger groups. Use stealth to avoid detection. If you are caught, melee weapons like a crowbar or a bat are your best bet.

3. First Encounter with the Freakers: Combat Tactics

The first major threat comes in the form of Freakers. While you've learned basic melee combat, this is where you'll need to start using your ranged weapons and strategize for survival.

Combat Tips:

- **Take Advantage of Stealth:** If you don't want to get caught in a horde of Freakers, try sneaking past them instead of engaging. Use the environment, like bushes and walls, to hide from their line of sight.
- **Use the Crossbow for Stealthy Kills:** If you've crafted a crossbow, use it for silent takedowns. The crossbow allows you to eliminate enemies without making noise, so you can sneak past undetected.
- **Exploit Weak Spots:** Aim for the head when you engage Freakers with firearms. Headshots deal more damage and will kill them more efficiently.
- **Use Melee When Ammunition is Low:** Save your ammo for tougher enemies. Melee combat is effective when you're facing

smaller groups of Freakers. If you're overwhelmed, retreat to a safe distance or find higher ground to regroup.

4. Objective: Reach the Safe House

The final objective of this mission is to reach a nearby safe house, which will act as a temporary shelter for Deacon. This is where you can take a breather, store resources, and craft essential items.

Objective Details:

- **Follow the Path to the Safe House:** The path is relatively straightforward, but be alert for any potential dangers. Keep your eyes peeled for Freakers hiding in the bushes or emerging from the woods.

- **Avoid Unnecessary Fights:** Since you've just begun the game, it's best to avoid engaging every enemy you come across. Prioritize reaching the safe house without attracting too much attention.

- **Check for Resources on the Way:** You can scavenge a few more resources as you make your way to the safe house. Don't rush every bit of scrap, gasoline, and gunpowder is valuable in these early stages.

5. Inside the Safe House: The First Night

Once you reach the safe house, you'll get a chance to pause the action and focus on survival. The safe house serves as a temporary base where you can rest, plan your next move, and manage your inventory.

What You Can Do Inside:

- **Rest and Recover:** This is your chance to heal up if you've been wounded during your trek. Use your crafted health kits to restore your health.

- **Crafting:** Use the crafting station inside the safe house to create important items, such as health kits, Molotovs, or even some basic weapons.

- **Plan Ahead:** Take stock of your inventory. If you've gathered enough materials, craft a few items to prepare for the next stage of the mission. You'll need to be well-equipped for the next challenges ahead.

6. Mission Completion: What You've Learned

By the end of "The Beginning of Survival," you will have completed several key objectives:

- You've learned how to navigate, scavenge, and fight against the Freakers.

- You've had your first real taste of combat and understood the importance of resource management.
  You've made it to your first safe house, where you can plan your next move in a somewhat safe environment.

Mission Tips:

- **Stay Quiet, Stay Safe:** Always be aware of your surroundings. Make use of stealth when possible, especially if you're low on ammo or health supplies.

- **Manage Your Resources:** You don't need to fight every enemy you come across. Conserve your ammunition and health kits for tougher encounters and focus on scavenging the essentials.

- **Adapt to the Environment:** Whether you're fighting Freakers, avoiding danger, or crafting new gear, always be flexible. The world of *Days Gone Remastered* is unforgiving, and adapting to each situation is key to survival.

6.2 MISSION 2: INTO THE HEART OF THE WILDERNESS

Mission 2, titled "Into the Heart of the Wilderness," takes the stakes higher and immerses you deeper into the wild, unforgiving landscape of *Days Gone Remastered*. This mission shifts the focus from learning the basics of survival to navigating a more challenging environment. As Deacon, you'll venture into more dangerous territory, deal with a wider range of enemies, and learn new tactics for combat and exploration. Here's a detailed walkthrough to guide you through the mission, offering insights and tips to ensure your success.

Mission Overview:

Mission Name: Into the Heart of the Wilderness
Location: Forested Areas / Abandoned Ranger Station
Objective: Travel through dangerous wilderness, confront new enemies, and find a way to deal with hostile factions and Freakers. You'll also need to gather additional resources to prepare for future encounters.

Mission Breakdown:

1. Starting Point: Setting the Stage

After the events of the first mission, "Into the Heart of the Wilderness" begins with Deacon receiving a request from a fellow survivor or a faction, asking for help. The mission introduces you to larger areas of the map, so exploration will be key.

What You'll Learn:

- **Navigating Through the Wilderness:** The game now introduces you to wider, more open areas. You'll need to learn how to travel efficiently, whether on foot or by bike, while watching out for Freakers and hostile humans.
- **Environmental Hazards:** The wilderness is home to natural dangers, such as cliffs, rivers, and dense woods, which you must navigate carefully. Also, be on the lookout for Freaker nests that may be scattered throughout.

2. Key Objective: Travel Through the Wilderness

The first real challenge of this mission is navigating through the wilderness while avoiding enemies and finding important locations, like abandoned ranger stations or old cabins.

Objective: **Reach**   **the**   **Ranger**   **Station**
You will be tasked with reaching a nearby ranger station that's believed to have supplies, intel, and shelter. Along the way, the mission introduces a variety of environmental factors that make the journey more dangerous.

Navigational Tips:
- **Use the Map and Waypoints:** Press the **Touchpad** (or **View Button**) to bring up the map and set a waypoint to your destination. The waypoints will keep you on track, even when navigating dense forests or uneven terrain.
- **Watch for Landmarks:** As you move through the wilderness, use natural landmarks like rivers, hills, or mountain ranges to help you orient yourself. The game's visual design makes it easy to get lost in the dense forest, so keep an eye on major landmarks to ensure you're headed in the right direction.
- **Take the Safe Route:** If you're venturing into a horde-infested area or a location with heavy resistance, take an alternate route. Avoiding large groups of enemies will conserve your resources and give you a better chance to survive.

3. Dealing with New Enemies: Humans and Freakers

As you explore deeper into the wilderness, you'll encounter more aggressive and diverse enemy types. In addition to the common Freakers, hostile human factions will make their first appearance, and they're just as dangerous if not more so than the infected.

Human Enemies:
- **Human Survivors:** These are hostile factions that have set up camps in the wilderness. They often use firearms and traps, making them more dangerous than the Freakers you've encountered so far. They'll attempt to ambush you, so be ready for a fight.

- **Combat Strategy:** Use cover to your advantage when facing human enemies. Hide behind trees, rocks, or structures to avoid getting hit. A headshot is always the quickest way to take them down, but take care of your ammo.

Freaker Encounters:

- **Stronger Freakers:** As you move deeper into the wilderness, you'll encounter more aggressive Freakers, including the ones with mutated characteristics. These enemies may be faster or stronger than what you faced in Mission 1, so be prepared for more intense battles.
- **Combat Strategy for Freakers:** Keep your distance when facing multiple Freakers. Use your ranged weapons like the rifle or crossbow to pick them off from afar. When surrounded, melee weapons like the axe or bat can help you clear them quickly without expending too much ammunition.

4. Objective: Secure the Ranger Station

Upon reaching the ranger station, the next task is to secure it and gather any necessary supplies or information. However, this area may be occupied by hostile humans or overrun with Freakers, requiring a combination of stealth and combat.

Objective Details:

- **Clear the Area:** When you arrive, take time to scout the surroundings. There may be enemies or Freakers nearby, and you'll need to eliminate them or sneak past them to get inside.
- **Inside the Station:** Once inside, loot the area for supplies, including ammunition, health kits, and crafting materials. Check for any clues that could lead to your next objective, such as maps, notes, or recordings.
- **Combat or Stealth:** If the station is heavily guarded, you can either engage the enemies head-on or take a stealthy approach. If you opt for combat, use the explosive items you've crafted, such as Molotov cocktails, to thin the group. For stealth, use your crossbow or silenced weapons to quietly eliminate targets.

Tips for Securing the Station:

- **Use the Environment:** As you enter the ranger station, use the buildings, fences, and other structures as cover to move undetected. Make sure to crouch and keep a low profile to avoid detection.
- **Check for Weaknesses:** Some enemies may be positioned near explosive barrels or gas cans. Shooting these can help clear out a group of enemies without wasting ammunition.

- **Lure Enemies Into Traps:** If you have crafted traps like bear traps or proximity mines, use them to set up ambushes for incoming enemies. This is particularly useful when you're low on ammo or want to avoid direct confrontation.

5. Objective: Gather Supplies and Information

Once the area is secured, you will need to gather supplies from the ranger station and search for important information that may help you in future missions.

Objective Details:

- **Loot Everything:** Make sure to search every room and building within the ranger station for ammo, materials, and health supplies. Even small items can make a huge difference in your next encounter.
- **Look for Clues:** You might also find maps or audio logs that provide more background on the situation and hint at where you should go next. This information will be valuable for planning your next steps and understanding the world around you.
- **Prepare for the Next Stage:** Make sure to craft and upgrade your equipment. Use the crafting stations at the ranger station to upgrade your weapons, create health kits, or craft more ammunition.

6. Returning to the Camp: Ending the Mission

Once you've gathered everything you need, it's time to return to the camp or base. However, the return trip won't be without its challenges. You may encounter more Freakers, ambushes, or difficult terrain along the way.

Objective: Return to the Camp

Use your bike to get back to safety, but be aware of potential threats. Keep an eye out for ambushes, especially from human factions that may have caught wind of your activities.

Return Tips:

- **Travel Quickly:** Keep your bike fueled and in good condition to make the return journey as smooth as possible. If you run low on fuel, stop to scavenge vehicles along the way.
- **Keep an Eye on the Horizon:** As you travel back, be alert for any large groups of enemies or horde spawns. Avoid them if possible, or prepare for combat if you can't avoid an encounter.
- **Don't Forget to Check Your Inventory:** Before returning, check your inventory and make sure you have enough health supplies, ammo, and crafting materials for the next mission. This preparation will help ensure you're ready for whatever comes next.

6.3 MISSION 3: FINDING ALLIES AND SUPPLIES

In *Days Gone Remastered*, the journey is as much about forming alliances and securing crucial supplies as it is about survival. Mission 3, "Finding Allies and Supplies," introduces you to new characters who will play pivotal roles in the story and provides an opportunity to stock up on essential resources to help you progress. The mission tests your ability to navigate through hostile territory while building connections that will aid you in future challenges.

Mission Overview:

Mission Name: Finding Allies and Supplies
Location: Abandoned Camp / Nearby Settlement
Objective: Locate allies in the wilderness, gather vital supplies for survival, and prepare for the upcoming journey.

Mission Breakdown:

1. Starting the Journey: The Search for Allies

At the start of this mission, Deacon receives information about a group of survivors who may have vital supplies and knowledge to help him on his journey. However, finding them won't be as easy as simply following the trail they are situated in an abandoned camp located deep in the wilderness.

What You'll Learn:

- **Meeting New Characters:** As part of this mission, you'll be introduced to key allies who will help you throughout the game. These characters may have missions of their own or provide essential resources that can aid your survival.

- **Navigating Through Hostile Territory:** Unlike earlier missions, this one takes you through areas where hostile human factions or heavily infected zones are more frequent. Knowing when to fight and when to flee is crucial.

2. Travel to the Abandoned Camp: A Hazardous Route

To begin this mission, you'll need to travel to a nearby abandoned camp, rumored to be the hiding place of the survivors. This route will take you through treacherous terrain filled with enemies, both human and Freakers.

Objective: Reach the Abandoned Camp

This part of the mission will test your navigation skills and ability to stay alert as you make your way through the wilderness.

Travel Tips:

- **Plan Your Route:** Open the map to set waypoints to ensure you're heading in the right direction. The wilderness can be a confusing place, with trees, mountains, and rivers blocking your path.

- **Watch for Human Factions:** As you approach the abandoned camp, there may be hostile human factions along the way. These groups can ambush you if you're not careful, so make use of stealth tactics to avoid detection when possible.
- **Gasoline for Your Bike:** The journey may take you through areas where gasoline is scarce. Ensure your bike has enough fuel before heading out, and keep an eye out for abandoned vehicles to siphon fuel along the way.

3. Entering the Abandoned Camp: First Contact with Allies

Upon arriving at the camp, you'll find it abandoned, but there may be clues left behind indicating where the survivors have gone. As you search the area, you will come across an unexpected ally or faction that can provide valuable information and supplies.

Objective: Investigate the Camp and Find Allies

Your goal is to locate someone who can help you, either by providing critical information or by joining your cause. However, not everyone in this post-apocalyptic world is friendly, so proceed with caution.

Tips for Exploration:
- **Search for Clues:** As you explore the camp, look for notes, messages, or signs of life that can point you to where the survivors went. Sometimes, the smallest detail can reveal a hidden stash or lead to a hidden ally.
- **Stealth Approach:** It's important to proceed cautiously. Human enemies may be hiding in the camp or nearby, waiting to ambush you. Use stealth to your advantage to avoid unnecessary combat.
- **Loot Everything:** Don't forget to loot the camp for supplies. This is a prime opportunity to stock up on health kits, ammunition, and crafting materials, which will be crucial for the upcoming missions.

4. Confrontation: Dealing with Hostile Factions

As you uncover more about the survivors, the situation takes an unexpected turn. Hostile factions or bandits may show up, having heard about your arrival. These factions could be looking for the same resources you've come to find, and a confrontation is inevitable.

Objective: Defeat Hostile Factions and Secure Supplies

You'll have to defend yourself and your allies from an incoming ambush. Use a combination of combat tactics, including ranged and melee attacks, to survive the assault.

Combat Strategy:
- **Use the Environment:** Look for cover behind rocks, vehicles, or buildings to protect yourself from enemy fire. Use your crossbow

or silenced weapons to pick off enemies quietly without alerting others to your position.

- **Molotovs and Explosives:** If you find yourself surrounded by enemies, use explosives or Molotov cocktails to create an area-of-effect attack. This is especially effective against large groups of enemies or when you're outnumbered.

- **Headshots and Weak Spots:** Aim for headshots to quickly eliminate enemies. Some human factions may be armored, so shoot for exposed weak points, such as their legs or head, to incapacitate them more effectively.

Escaping the Conflict:

- **Escape Route:** If things go south and you're outnumbered, consider retreating. Your bike will be crucial for a quick getaway. Look for an escape route and be ready to flee if necessary.

- **Strategic Retreat:** Always know where your exit points are. If the fight turns against you, make sure to have a plan to retreat without getting cornered.

5. Securing Supplies: The Aftermath

Once the hostile faction has been dealt with, it's time to secure the supplies. The camp should have valuable resources, from ammunition to health kits, and you'll need to collect as much as you can.

Objective: Loot the Camp for Supplies

After the fight, take the time to thoroughly search the camp. Even if the battle was intense, don't forget to gather everything you can this is your chance to restock and prepare for the next phase of your journey.

Supply Checklist:

- **Ammunition:** Make sure you have enough ammo for your firearms and crossbow. Ammunition can be scarce, so only use it when necessary.

- **Health Kits:** Craft and gather health kits to ensure you're ready for any future fights.

- **Crafting Materials:** Collect scrap, nails, gunpowder, and other materials to craft traps, explosives, and more.

- **Fuel for the Bike:** Don't forget to siphon fuel from any abandoned vehicles to make sure your bike is ready for the next leg of your journey.

6. Returning to the Camp: Reporting Your Findings

With the supplies in hand and the hostile faction neutralized, you'll need to return to the camp and report your findings. The next part of the mission will likely involve sharing the information you've gathered and using it to plan your next move.

Objective: Return to the Safehouse or Base

Head back to the designated base to report the situation. This is also a good time to craft new items, upgrade your gear, and strategize for the next phase of your journey.

Mission Tips and Strategies:

- **Use Stealth to Your Advantage:** Always approach new areas cautiously. Use stealth when necessary to avoid alerting enemies to your presence. Crossbows and silenced weapons are your best tools for stealthy takedowns.

- **Conserve Resources:** You'll face many challenges in the wilderness, so try not to waste resources like ammunition and health kits. Save them for tougher situations, and use melee weapons or stealth when possible.

- **Upgrade as You Go:** As you gather supplies and progress, take the time to upgrade your gear. Whether it's improving your bike's fuel efficiency or upgrading your weapons, these improvements will make your journey much easier.

- **Know When to Fight and When to Flee:** If you're outnumbered or low on resources, it's better to retreat than to risk a costly fight. Always plan your escape routes and be ready to flee if things go wrong.

6.4 MISSION 4: CONFRONTING THE FREAKER HORDES

Mission 4, titled **"Confronting the Freaker Hordes,"** ramps up the intensity in *Days Gone Remastered*. This mission challenges you to face the overwhelming force of the Freaker hordes, one of the game's most intimidating and dangerous enemies. While previous missions may have prepared you for smaller skirmishes, this mission forces you to take on large-scale confrontations with multiple Freakers at once. With the right preparation, strategy, and tactical combat, you can survive this terrifying encounter. Let's dive into the mission's objectives, breakdowns, and tips to help you succeed.

Mission Overview:

Mission Name: Confronting the Freaker Hordes
Location: Freaker Infested Areas / Hordes Lair
Objective: Engage in combat with a Freaker horde, survive the encounter,

and clear out the infestation. This mission tests your combat, resource management, and strategic planning abilities.

Mission Breakdown:

1. Preparing for the Horde: Essential Setup

Before you even think about confronting the Freaker hordes, preparation is key. This mission will force you to use everything you've learned so far: your combat skills, resource management, and tactical positioning.

What You'll Need:

- **A Full Arsenal:** Ensure that you have a diverse selection of weapons for the encounter. A combination of ranged weapons (like rifles or shotguns) and melee weapons (like an axe or crowbar) will be crucial. You'll need to deal with both individual Freakers and large swarms.
  Molotov Cocktails and Pipe Bombs: These explosives are your go-to weapons for large groups. Their area-of-effect damage can thin out the horde quickly, giving you breathing room. Make sure you have plenty in your inventory.

- **Crossbow with Bolts:** The crossbow is ideal for picking off individual Freakers from a distance without making noise. This can help you manage the smaller stragglers in the horde without alerting others.

- **Health Kits and Stamina Boosters:** The sheer chaos of the horde will make it easy to take damage. Keep your health topped up with health kits and have stamina boosters ready for when you need to run or fight longer.

Pre-Mission Tips:

- **Scavenge for Supplies:** Prior to initiating the encounter, search the area around the horde's lair. You'll want to gather scrap, fuel, and medical supplies to ensure you have enough materials for crafting and surviving the battle.

- **Upgrade Your Bike:** Make sure your bike is fueled and upgraded with the best equipment. You might need it for a quick getaway or to use as a distraction during the horde encounter.

2. Tracking the Horde's Lair

To confront the Freaker hordes, you'll need to first find their lair. Freaker nests are often located in areas like caves, abandoned structures, or large settlements. These nests are breeding grounds for the Freakers, and taking them out will significantly reduce the horde's numbers in that area.

Objective: Locate the Horde's Nest

The horde's lair is your first target. It can sometimes be hidden in plain sight, so you'll need to explore the environment thoroughly.

Tips for Finding the Horde's Nest:

- **Look for Signs of Activity:** Watch for signs of heavy Freaker activity, such as large groups moving in one direction, noises, or trails of destruction.

- **Listen for Sounds:** Freaker nests often make low, unsettling sounds, and you may hear them before you see them. Use these audio cues to guide you toward the lair.

- **Map Awareness:** Mark the location of the nest on your map so you can navigate there more efficiently. The world can be vast, so using waypoints will ensure you stay on track.

3. Confronting the Horde: The Battle Begins

Once you've found the lair, the mission transitions into a full-fledged battle. At this point, you must engage the Freakers and survive their relentless attacks. This is where your combat and survival skills will be put to the test.

Objective: Clear the Freaker Horde

The main objective of this mission is to eliminate the horde by either killing the Freakers directly or destroying their nest. You have two options: fight the horde head-on or try to destroy the nest to weaken the enemies.

Combat Tips for Confronting the Horde:

- **Set Traps:** Before engaging the horde, use the environment to your advantage. Set traps in key choke points bear traps, mines, or Molotov cocktails placed in strategic locations can help you deal massive damage to the horde.

- **Use Fire and Explosives:** Molotov cocktails and pipe bombs are extremely effective in clearing out large groups. When the horde is clustered together, throw explosives to cause maximum damage.

- **Keep Moving:** The horde can quickly surround you if you're not careful. Keep your movement unpredictable and avoid staying in one spot for too long. Use the high ground or nearby structures to get a better vantage point and reduce the number of Freakers attacking from all sides.

- **Headshots and Precision:** While aiming for the head isn't necessary for clearing the entire horde, it's important when you're dealing with tougher Freakers. Headshots can also help you quickly kill any stragglers or more dangerous enemies within the group.

Managing Ammo and Health:

- **Conserve Ammo:** Don't waste your ammunition on small groups of Freakers or when you can easily dispatch them with melee combat. Save your firearms for larger threats or more difficult situations.
- **Use Health Kits Wisely:** Freakers will swarm you, and you'll take damage throughout the battle. Use health kits when you're critically low on health, but don't wait until the last moment to heal. Stamina boosters will also come in handy when you need to sprint away from danger.

4. Destroying the Horde's Nest: Weakening the Enemy

While fighting the horde is important, you can also eliminate the source of the problem by destroying the Freaker nest. These nests are the breeding grounds for the Freakers, and taking them out will stop the constant flow of new enemies into the battle.

Objective: Destroy the Freaker Nest

The nest may be hidden in a building, cave, or under a large pile of debris. Once you find it, you'll need to destroy it using fire, explosives, or your firearm.

Nest Destruction Tips:

- **Use Molotovs:** The best way to destroy a Freaker nest is by setting it on fire. Throw Molotov cocktails directly into the nest to set it ablaze. The flames will cause it to collapse, destroying the nest and reducing the number of Freakers in the area.
- **Use Firearms for Precision:** If you can't get close enough to throw a Molotov, you can shoot the nest with a high-powered weapon. Rifles or shotguns are effective for this, but make sure to keep an eye on your surroundings, as shooting may attract more Freakers.

5. Surviving the Aftermath: Completing the Mission

Once you've destroyed the nest and cleared the area, your next task is to leave the location safely. However, the battle doesn't always end with the nest's destruction. A few Freakers may still be lurking around, or new groups may arrive in search of fresh prey.

Objective: Escape Safely

After completing the mission objectives, use your bike to leave the area. Be prepared for any last-minute ambushes or Freaker swarms trying to close in on you.

Post-Mission Tips:

- **Check for Remaining Threats:** After you clear the nest and fight off the horde, take a moment to scan the area for remaining threats. These might include stray Freakers or hostile humans trying to take advantage of the situation.

- **Return to Safety:** Head back to your safe house or base to regroup. This mission likely took a lot of your resources, so you'll want to restock and prepare for the next challenge.

Mission Tips and Strategies:

- **Be Patient:** Fighting a horde isn't a race. Take your time to set up traps, gather resources, and clear out enemies in waves. You don't need to rush into battle.

- **Adapt to the Situation:** Depending on the size of the horde, you may need to switch tactics. If you're overwhelmed, retreat and find higher ground. If you're doing well, use your explosives to finish them off quickly.

- **Upgrade Your Gear:** Before confronting the horde, ensure your gear is in top condition. Upgrade your weapons, bike, and equipment to ensure you have the best tools for the job.

CHAPTER 7: SECRETS AND COLLECTIBLES

7.1 HIDDEN COLLECTIBLES: WHERE TO FIND THEM

In *Days Gone Remastered*, the world is full of secrets, hidden collectibles, and Easter eggs that enhance the gameplay experience. Whether you're a completionist trying to collect every item or simply looking to uncover the mysteries of the game's expansive world, this chapter will guide you through some of the most valuable hidden gems you can find. From collectibles that deepen the narrative to secret locations that reveal new challenges, this guide will help you discover everything the game has to offer.

Days Gone Remastered is rich with hidden collectibles scattered throughout the world. These items are not only fun to find, but they also provide additional lore, backstory, and rewards that enhance the overall experience. Collecting them all can be a challenge, but the rewards are well worth the effort.

Here's where you can find some of the most important collectibles hidden in the wilderness:

1. Nero Research Stations

Nero Research Stations are one of the most significant collectibles in *Days Gone Remastered*, as they provide both lore and important resources. These stations contain data records, useful crafting materials, and Nero injectors that increase Deacon's stats. Finding all of these stations is a major part of the game's exploration challenge.

Where to Find Them:

- **Location Tip:** Nero Research Stations are scattered across the map and usually require you to venture into dangerous territory. They are often located near military installations, abandoned camps, or even secluded areas surrounded by Freakers.
- **Look for the Markers:** Nero Research Stations are marked on your map with a red icon, but they can be tricky to reach due to the large number of enemies in the area. Look for nearby entrances or hidden paths to avoid large groups of enemies.
- **Be Prepared for a Fight:** These stations often have hostile human factions or Freakers guarding them. Make sure to have ample ammunition and health supplies before entering.

2. Audio Logs

Throughout the world, you'll find audio logs that tell stories from the pre-apocalypse era. These logs provide valuable insight into the world before the outbreak and help build the game's backstory. Collecting these can deepen your understanding of the narrative and the characters.

Where to Find Them:

- **Location Tip:** Audio logs can be found in various locations, including abandoned vehicles, small camps, and inside structures like ranger stations and old houses.
- **Pay Attention to the Environment:** Audio logs are often hidden in places you wouldn't expect, such as behind crates, under tables, or tucked away in cabinets. Make sure to search every room or area thoroughly to uncover these hidden gems.

3. Collectible Cards

Collectible cards, though not as critical as other collectibles, can still offer unique rewards. These cards, featuring various characters and factions from the *Days Gone* universe, add an extra layer of immersion to the game.

Where to Find Them:

- **Location Tip:** These cards are often located in less obvious places, such as on the shelves of abandoned stores, inside random crates, or hidden among piles of debris. They may also be dropped by enemies or found in secret compartments within larger structures.
- **Rarer Cards:** Some cards can only be unlocked by completing specific missions or challenges. These cards often offer special lore entries that shed light on the history of the world or specific factions.

4. Backpack Locations

Backpacks are a type of collectible that contains useful supplies, including ammo, crafting materials, and health kits. While these items are not as rare or lore-rich as some of the others, finding every backpack can make your survival much easier.

Where to Find Them:

- **Location Tip:** Backpacks are scattered across the world and can often be found on enemies, abandoned cars, and inside buildings. They may appear in both obvious and hidden spots, so be sure to check around corners and under structures.
- **Exploration:** Some backpacks are located in off-the-beaten-path areas or hard-to-reach locations. Use your bike and park it nearby to save time when collecting backpacks in remote areas.

5. Story Items (Posters, Diaries, and Notes)

Throughout your journey, you'll encounter various story-related collectibles such as posters, diaries, and notes that flesh out the world's history and the lives of the characters. These items serve as a great way to enhance the narrative experience.

Where to Find Them:

- **Location Tip:** Look in areas where people may have lived or worked, such as homes, shops, and bunkers. You can find these items on walls, tables, and other high-traffic areas.
- **Check for Hidden Rooms:** Some story items are tucked away in hidden rooms or behind locked doors. Ensure that you have the proper skills or tools to unlock and gain access to these locations.

7.2 SECRET LOCATIONS AND EASTER EGGS

One of the most enjoyable aspects of *Days Gone Remastered* is the variety of secret locations and Easter eggs hidden throughout the game world. These special locations reward curiosity and often offer unique items, interesting lore, or humorous references that add personality to the game. Here are a few secret spots and Easter eggs you should keep an eye out for.

1. Secret Bunkers and Caves

Days Gone Remastered has numerous bunkers and caves hidden throughout the world, offering rare supplies, weapons, and sometimes a break from the chaos. These hidden locations often require some exploration, and in many cases, the entrance is cleverly concealed.

Where to Find Them:

- **Look for Unmarked Locations:** Some bunkers and caves are not marked on your map, so you'll need to keep an eye out for natural landmarks. Look for cave openings, rock formations, or large hidden doors that you might otherwise miss.
- **Underground Entrances:** Some bunkers have underground entrances hidden behind bushes or within dilapidated structures. Investigate any suspiciously intact buildings to discover hidden access points.

2. Hidden Freaker Nests

Freaker nests are one of the more dangerous yet rewarding secret locations. By clearing out these nests, you'll prevent Freakers from respawning in certain areas and earn a variety of rewards, including loot and progression toward achieving a safer environment.

Where to Find Them:

- **Look for Signs of Disturbance:** Freaker nests are often found in caves, large abandoned buildings, or even under bridges. You'll notice the environment will change becoming more hostile with signs of Freaker activity, such as piles of debris, human remains, or loud noises.

- **Environmental Cues:** Some nests glow with a sickly light or have a distinctive smell. Look for visual and auditory cues as you explore, and always be prepared for an ambush when dealing with these areas.

3. Hidden Easter Eggs

In true open-world fashion, *Days Gone Remastered* features several fun Easter eggs that pay homage to popular culture, other games, and the developers themselves. These Easter eggs provide moments of humor and surprise, adding an extra layer of enjoyment for dedicated players.

Notable Easter Eggs:

- **The 'Shamblers' Tribute:** A nod to classic horror games, you can find references to other famous franchises within the world of *Days Gone Remastered*, like hidden posters or graffiti that allude to familiar characters or games.
- **The Waffle House:** A humorous Easter egg, found in a small diner in the wilderness, contains a series of waffles and messages referencing popular media. This quirky location gives players something to chuckle at as they venture through the game.

4. Hidden Treasure Locations

Scattered throughout the game are hidden treasure caches, some of which contain high-end weapons, rare crafting materials, or unique upgrades for your bike. Finding these treasures requires keen observation and a willingness to explore every nook and cranny of the environment.

Where to Find Them:

- **On the Map:** Occasionally, treasure caches are marked with an icon on the map, but they might require a bit of extra effort to access, such as completing a mini-challenge or overcoming an environmental obstacle.
- **Look for Abandoned Settlements:** Treasure caches are often found in deserted homes, camps, or military outposts. Explore these locations thoroughly, even checking behind large rocks, inside locked boxes, or under debris.

5. Hidden Vehicles and Bikes

Throughout the map, you can find hidden vehicles and bikes that provide unique advantages, whether it's a faster bike, one with more storage, or simply a better aesthetic. These hidden bikes are often well-hidden but provide a great incentive for players to explore every corner of the game world.

Where to Find Them:

- **Look for Abandoned Biker Camps:** Some of the best bikes are located in old biker camps, surrounded by Freakers or hostile humans. Be prepared for a fight to claim the bike, but the reward is worth the risk.
- **Special Locations:** Some bikes are hidden in remote areas or tucked away in places where you wouldn't expect to find them. Make sure to check vehicles along your journey for any that may hold a surprise.

7.3 UNLOCKING HIDDEN FEATURES

Days Gone Remastered is packed with hidden features that can significantly enhance the gameplay experience. Some of these features are not immediately available, requiring specific actions or accomplishments before they are unlocked. From secret modes to game-changing abilities, unlocking these features adds replayability and new challenges. In this section, we'll explore some of the most exciting hidden features in *Days Gone Remastered* and how you can unlock them.

1. Unlocking the Survival Mode

Survival Mode is a highly challenging feature that increases the difficulty of the game, testing your survival skills to the limit. It modifies the game's mechanics, making resources scarcer and enemies more aggressive. This mode is perfect for players looking for a real challenge.

How to Unlock Survival Mode:

- **Complete the Main Story:** To unlock Survival Mode, you must first finish the main storyline. This ensures you're familiar with the core mechanics before facing a much harder challenge.
- **Activate in the Main Menu:** Once you've completed the story, you'll be able to select Survival Mode from the main menu. This mode will alter the way you interact with the game world, forcing you to manage your resources more carefully and deal with tougher enemies.

What to Expect in Survival Mode:

- **Limited Resources:** Ammo and health kits will be much harder to come by, requiring you to scavenge more thoughtfully and manage your supplies effectively.

- **Freakers and Enemies:** Freakers and human factions will be far more numerous and aggressive. You'll need to adapt your strategy, utilizing stealth and traps to survive.
- **Increased Difficulty:** Everything from combat to exploration will be more punishing, making each decision critical to your survival.

2. Unlocking the Custom Bike Mods

One of the most satisfying features in *Days Gone Remastered* is the ability to customize and upgrade your bike. While you can enhance your bike's performance and appearance throughout the game, there are special mods that can only be unlocked under certain conditions.

How to Unlock Custom Bike Mods:

- **Reach Specific Trust Levels with Factions:** Factions like the Rippers, Lost Lake, and others will offer bike mods once you've earned enough trust with them. The higher your trust level, the better mods you can unlock.
- **Complete Challenges or Objectives:** Some mods are tied to completing specific challenges, such as clearing Freaker nests, surviving certain horde encounters, or completing timed objectives. Keep an eye out for these special objectives in your quest log.
- **Upgrade Your Bike in the Shop:** Once you've unlocked these mods, visit bike mechanic stations where you can install them to increase your bike's speed, durability, and fuel efficiency. Some mods can even change the aesthetics of your bike, giving it a more personalized look.

Special Mods:

- **Performance Mods:** These mods increase your bike's speed, handling, and fuel efficiency, making it easier to outrun enemies or travel long distances.
- **Cosmetic Mods:** These mods change the appearance of your bike, adding custom paint jobs, decals, and other visual upgrades that make your bike stand out from others.

3. Unlocking New Weapon Types

As you progress through *Days Gone Remastered*, you'll have the opportunity to unlock new weapons that can be used to deal with tougher enemies. Some of these weapons are hidden behind specific achievements or require you to complete certain side missions.

How to Unlock New Weapons:

- **Complete Special Tasks or Challenges:** Weapons like the powerful **M60 Machine Gun** or **Crossbow** can be unlocked by completing specific challenges, such as taking down large hordes or clearing out certain areas.
- **Reach Faction Trust Levels:** Some weapons, especially unique firearms, are locked behind specific faction trust levels. As you gain trust, new weapons will become available at various stores or crafting stations.
- **Story Progression:** Certain advanced weapons are unlocked as you progress through the main story. For example, high-powered sniper rifles or explosive weapons are often made available later in the game.

Weapons to Look For:

- **Melee Weapons:** More powerful melee options like the **Sledgehammer** or **Machete** can be unlocked after defeating certain enemies or completing specific side objectives.
- **Ranged Weapons:** Unlock advanced firearms such as **silenced sniper rifles** or the **compound bow** by completing tough side missions or upgrading your trust with factions.

4. Unlocking the New Game Plus Mode

New Game Plus (NG+ mode) is a special feature that allows you to replay the game with all your progress, including weapons, skills, and upgrades, carried over into a higher difficulty setting. This mode is perfect for players who want to experience the game again but with a fresh challenge.

How to Unlock New Game Plus Mode:

- **Finish the Main Story:** To unlock NG+, you must complete the main story of *Days Gone Remastered*. Once you finish the game, you'll be able to start a new playthrough with your existing gear and progress intact.
- **Choose Your Difficulty:** NG+ mode comes with an increased difficulty level, making enemies harder to kill, resources more scarce, and survival more challenging. You can choose the difficulty setting that suits your desired experience.

What Changes in NG+:

- **Increased Enemy Difficulty:** Freakers, hostile humans, and other enemies become more aggressive, and their AI becomes more unpredictable.
- **Carry Over Progress:** All your unlocked gear, abilities, and upgrades carry over into the new playthrough, allowing you to approach challenges with greater power.

- **New Rewards:** NG+ also offers special rewards for completing the game a second time, including rare items, collectibles, and even new story elements or challenges.

7.4 ACHIEVING SECRET ENDINGS

In *Days Gone Remastered*, there are several secret endings that can only be unlocked by fulfilling certain requirements or making specific choices throughout the game. These endings offer a different perspective on the story and reveal additional layers of the narrative. Here's how you can unlock them and what they entail.

1. The True Survivor Ending

The True Survivor Ending is one of the most rewarding and complex secret endings in the game. It's unlocked by making specific choices and completing various side missions that test your commitment to surviving and protecting those you care about.

How to Unlock the True Survivor Ending:

- **Complete All Major Side Missions:** Focus on completing all major side missions, especially those that involve saving survivors, clearing out Freaker nests, and helping key characters in the game.
- **Maximize Faction Trust:** Build strong relationships with the factions, completing their objectives and earning their trust. This is crucial for accessing special weapons, supplies, and story events.
- **Make Key Decisions:** Throughout the game, Deacon will be faced with tough decisions that affect the story's outcome. Choose to help others and sacrifice for the greater good, rather than choosing selfish options.

What You'll Experience in the Ending:

- **A Different Resolution:** This ending provides a more hopeful and conclusive resolution to the story, offering closure to Deacon's journey and the people he's met along the way.
- **Rewarding Story Depth:** You'll get additional backstory and context about the characters you helped, as well as insights into the future of the world after the Freaker outbreak.

2. The Dark Ending

The Dark Ending is a more tragic conclusion to *Days Gone Remastered*, where Deacon chooses to prioritize his personal goals over the greater good. This ending reveals a darker side of the protagonist and gives players a glimpse into the emotional toll the world has taken on Deacon.

How to Unlock the Dark Ending:

- **Make Selfish Choices:** Throughout the game, make decisions that put your needs first. Choose to focus on personal goals over helping others, and avoid completing side missions that benefit the survivors.
- **Ignore Key Characters:** While building alliances is crucial for the True Survivor Ending, the Dark Ending is unlocked by distancing yourself from certain characters, focusing instead on completing your journey alone.

What You'll Experience in the Ending:

- **A Bleak Resolution:** The Dark Ending provides a somber conclusion, with Deacon's isolation and emotional struggles taking center stage.
- **Story Consequences:** Some of the characters you've encountered may meet grim fates, and the aftermath of the Freaker outbreak is less hopeful.

3. The Ultimate Survivor Ending

The Ultimate Survivor Ending is the most challenging and rewarding ending in *Days Gone Remastered*. It requires you to survive the longest without dying or losing too much health, as well as making choices that are selfless and heroic.

How to Unlock the Ultimate Survivor Ending:

- **Complete Hardcore Challenges:** Engage in the hardest difficulty settings, and complete all the most difficult side missions, like clearing large hordes or surviving in the most dangerous areas of the map.
- **Make Heroic Decisions:** Throughout the story, prioritize saving others and securing the future of the survivors over your own well-being.

What You'll Experience in the Ending:

- **Heroic Conclusion:** Deacon emerges as a true hero, having made significant sacrifices and decisions to save the world around him. The ending showcases the growth of Deacon from a lone survivor to a dedicated protector.
- **Exclusive Rewards:** The Ultimate Survivor Ending comes with special rewards, such as rare gear, collectibles, and secret dialogue options that reflect your heroic journey.

CHAPTER 8: ACHIEVEMENTS AND TROPHIES

8.1 PLATINUM TROPHY GUIDE

In *Days Gone Remastered*, achieving all the trophies is a rewarding experience that showcases your mastery of the game. Whether you're aiming for the elusive Platinum Trophy or looking to complete every challenge, this chapter is designed to help you unlock every achievement and trophy the game has to offer. With a mix of skill-based tasks, exploration, and completing side missions, the trophies are as varied as the gameplay itself. We'll break down the steps to unlock the Platinum Trophy, as well as highlight missable achievements and how to get them.

The Platinum Trophy in *Days Gone Remastered* is a prestigious achievement that signifies you've completed every major task the game has to offer. To unlock this coveted trophy, you'll need to earn all other trophies in the game, which includes completing all story missions, side objectives, and challenges.

Here's your roadmap to earning the Platinum Trophy:

1. Completing the Main Story

The backbone of the trophy list is completing the main storyline. While the game's story offers plenty of excitement and emotional depth, you'll need to follow Deacon's journey from start to finish to unlock key trophies.

Main Story Trophies to Unlock:

- **Story Completion:** Every time you finish a major storyline arc, you'll unlock a new trophy. These are mostly tied to completing specific chapters of the game, such as defeating particular bosses or reaching major plot points.
- **Trophy Example:** "Out of the Fire" – Earned after completing the major climax of the main story.

2. Completing Side Missions and Challenges

Aside from the main story, side missions and challenges are crucial for unlocking the Platinum Trophy. These missions will test your combat skills, stealth abilities, and resourcefulness. Completing all side missions, including Freaker nests, clearing ambush camps, and helping other survivors, is necessary for the Platinum.

Key Side Missions to Complete:

- **Nero Research Stations:** Collecting all Nero injectors and data entries is essential for both progression and trophies.

- **Horde Battles:** Clearing all Freaker hordes around the world is a time-consuming but rewarding challenge that will grant you several trophies.

Challenge Trophies to Unlock:

- **Horde Hunter:** Defeat a specific number of Freaker hordes scattered across the map.
- **Heartbreaker:** Clear out every Freaker nest, one of the more challenging side objectives.

3. Collectibles and Exploration

Exploration and finding collectibles is another core component of *Days Gone Remastered*'s trophy list. There are several hidden items and locations that you must discover to achieve 100% completion.

What You Need to Find:

- **Collectible Cards:** Hidden throughout the world, these cards unlock additional lore and are an essential part of your completion journey.
- **Audio Logs and Diaries:** Unlocking all audio logs and diaries scattered throughout the map adds more lore and gives you another important set of trophies.

Trophy Example:

- **The Collector:** Unlock all collectibles, including cards, audio logs, and other hidden items.

4. Difficulty-Specific Trophies

If you're looking to test your skills further, there are difficulty-specific trophies that require completing the game on higher difficulty settings. These trophies challenge your combat prowess and survival instincts.

Difficulty Trophies to Unlock:

- **Survivalist:** Complete the game on the hardest difficulty, requiring perfect resource management and combat strategies.

5. Miscellaneous Achievements

There are several smaller trophies that require you to do specific things, such as executing a certain number of headshots, completing unique feats of strength, or engaging in specific gameplay mechanics.

Examples Include:

- **Gunslinger:** Get a certain number of kills with different types of guns.
- **Upgraded:** Fully upgrade your bike or gear.

8.2 MISSABLE ACHIEVEMENTS AND HOW TO GET THEM

Days Gone Remastered offers a rich world to explore, but there are a few achievements that are tied to specific moments or choices. These missable trophies can easily be missed if you're not paying close attention to the game's narrative or optional objectives. In this section, we'll walk you through the most critical missable achievements and how to ensure you unlock them.

1. Survivor of the Lost Lake

This trophy is unlocked by completing a specific set of missions for the Lost Lake camp, one of the key survivor factions in the game. It's important to keep track of your faction missions, as missing out on a few will prevent you from unlocking this trophy.

How to Unlock It:

- **Mission Order:** Pay attention to when the Lost Lake faction missions become available. You must complete all their main missions as well as some optional ones.
- **Missable Tip:** If you miss one of the faction missions early on, you won't be able to earn this trophy during your first playthrough. It's advisable to keep an eye on the mission board at the Lost Lake camp to ensure you finish everything required.

2. Blood on the Road

This missable achievement involves taking down a specific number of human enemies using your bike. It's easy to overlook this task, especially when focusing on Freakers, but completing this will add another trophy to your collection.

How to Unlock It:

- **Required Action:** Use your bike to ram and kill enemies as you progress through the game. This must be done with human enemies, not Freakers.
- **Missable Tip:** If you avoid engaging with human factions on your bike or rely on combat, you may miss this trophy. Make sure to get into the habit of using your bike in combat for ramming or running over enemies.

3. It's Just a Flesh Wound

This achievement requires you to defeat a specific type of Freaker, the **Rager** (an infected Freaker variant). This encounter is a one-time story event, and if you miss the chance, you won't be able to earn the trophy during the rest of the playthrough.

How to Unlock It:

- **Key Moment:** During a story mission, you'll face off against a Rager. Take this opportunity to defeat it, as it's the only time in the game you can earn this trophy.
- **Missable Tip:** Be sure to pay attention to the story and the type of Freakers you encounter during your missions. If you accidentally skip the opportunity, you may need to replay the mission to earn the trophy.

4. The Heart of the Freaker

This trophy is tied to clearing all the Freaker nests in the game, and it's easy to miss out on some if you're too focused on the main story.

How to Unlock It:

- **Exploration Required:** As you progress through the game, you'll encounter Freaker nests that need to be cleared. Clearing them will reward you with crafting materials, but more importantly, it's required to unlock this trophy.
- **Missable Tip:** Keep track of the nests you've cleared. If you skip too many of these side objectives, you may find yourself unable to unlock this trophy by the end of the game. Check the map and make sure you've visited all the marked locations.

5. Heartbreaker

This achievement is unlocked by completing a specific side mission involving a dangerous encounter with a massive Freaker horde. This side mission can be easily missed if you don't go out of your way to clear the horde locations early.

How to Unlock It:

- **Key Challenge:** After reaching a certain point in the game, you'll be tasked with clearing a specific horde of Freakers in a large area. This side mission requires you to destroy the nest and eliminate the horde.
- **Missable Tip:** If you continue with the main story and ignore the side missions, you could easily miss this opportunity. Make sure to return to the areas with horde nests and clear them when they become available.

6. The Collector's Dream

This missable trophy requires you to collect all the collectible cards scattered throughout the game world. While some are easy to find, others are tucked away in hidden locations or locked behind difficult side missions. Missing any of these cards will prevent you from unlocking this trophy.

How to Unlock It:

- **Find All Collectibles:** You must gather every single collectible card scattered throughout the world. These cards are often hidden in hard-to-reach places, so be sure to explore every nook and cranny.
- **Missable Tip:** The key to unlocking this trophy is paying attention to the collectible cards you find early on. As the game progresses, some areas will be blocked off, and you won't be able to go back. Keep a checklist of the collectible cards and check them off as you go.

8.3 BEST STRATEGIES FOR EARNING TROPHIES

Earning trophies in *Days Gone Remastered* is not only about completing the main story but also about mastering the various systems the game offers, including combat, exploration, and resource management. Whether you're aiming for a specific trophy or just want to maximize your overall achievements, this section will provide you with the best strategies to efficiently earn trophies and unlock all the rewards the game has to offer.

1. Prioritize Side Missions Early On

One of the easiest ways to earn trophies is by focusing on side missions early in the game. Many of the trophies require you to complete these optional objectives, including clearing Freaker nests, helping survivors, and clearing ambush camps. By engaging with these side missions from the beginning, you'll increase your chances of unlocking trophies while also leveling up your skills and gathering valuable resources.

Tips:

- **Track All Side Missions:** Always check your mission log and be sure to mark side objectives on your map. Focusing on these early on can help you unlock several trophies, including those related to clearing nests, horde challenges, and helping different factions.
- **Concentrate on Easy Side Missions:** Early in the game, try to focus on the simpler side missions, as they will give you easier trophies to earn, like "Helping Hand" or "Freaker Hunter."

2. Master Stealth for Stealth-Related Trophies

Stealth is a crucial mechanic in *Days Gone Remastered* and is tied to several trophies. Whether you need to sneak past enemies or silently eliminate them, mastering stealth will help you earn trophies like "Silent But Deadly" and others tied to non-lethal takedowns.

Tips:

- **Move Slowly and Crouch:** Always crouch and move slowly when attempting stealth. Use **L2 (LT)** to crouch and stay hidden. Avoid sprinting when near enemies.
- **Use Stealth Takedowns:** Use your crossbow, silenced weapons, or melee weapons to silently take down enemies. These actions often lead to trophies like "Ghost of the Wilderness."
- **Use Distractions Effectively:** Throw rocks, bottles, or use other objects to distract enemies, allowing you to sneak past or line up stealthy takedowns.

3. Combat Trophies: Focus on Specific Enemy Weaknesses

Many of the game's combat-related trophies are based on defeating specific enemy types, whether Freakers, humans, or large hordes. Understanding enemy behavior and weaknesses will allow you to efficiently earn combat trophies, like "Sharp Shooter" and "Horde Hunter."

Tips:

- **Headshots Are Key:** For trophies related to kills, aim for headshots. This applies to both Freakers and human enemies. Using your rifles or crossbows will help you achieve "Headshot Expert."
- **Learn Enemy Patterns:** Observe the attack patterns of Freakers and human factions. Knowing when to strike, when to dodge, and when to use explosives will help you take down enemies faster and unlock related combat trophies.
- **Tackle Hordes Efficiently:** Clearing out horde locations is tied to several trophies, including "Horde Hunter." Ensure you have a mix of explosives, traps, and a good weapon for long-range combat to help you tackle these challenges.

4. Focus on Resource Management for Collectible Trophies

Collecting everything from crafting materials to collectibles is a large part of the game's trophies. You'll need to manage your resources well to both unlock trophies and prepare for harder missions later on. Proper resource management will help you unlock trophies related to crafting, gathering, and upgrading.

Tips:

- **Craft Consistently:** Craft health kits, Molotov cocktails, and other items as you go along. Not only will this prepare you for combat, but it will also unlock crafting-related trophies.
- **Loot Everything:** Scavenge all abandoned vehicles, camps, and structures. Many trophies are tied to the items you find, including collectible cards, audio logs, and scraps.

- **Upgrade Your Gear:** Some trophies are linked to upgrading your gear. Regularly upgrade your bike, weapons, and Deacon's abilities to unlock these trophies.

5. Use New Game Plus (NG+) for Additional Challenges

Once you've completed the main story, *Days Gone Remastered* offers a New Game Plus mode, where you can carry over your progress and unlock even more difficult trophies. This mode lets you tackle the game with all of your weapons, skills, and upgrades, but at a higher difficulty level, offering a chance to earn tougher trophies.

Tips:

- **Complete on Higher Difficulty:** NG+ brings with it tougher enemies and more complex challenges. Completing the game on harder difficulties is linked to trophies like "Survivalist" and "Hardcore."
- **Use NG+ for Missed Trophies:** If you missed some trophies during your first playthrough, New Game Plus offers an excellent opportunity to get them while enjoying the game again.

8.4 EARNING ALL COLLECTIBLE TROPHIES

Collectible trophies are one of the most rewarding aspects of *Days Gone Remastered*. They not only provide insight into the game's lore but also offer a tangible sense of accomplishment. Whether you're collecting cards, clearing out Freaker nests, or gathering hidden collectibles, there are many trophies tied to discovering everything the game world has to offer. In this section, we'll break down the best strategies to earn every collectible trophy in the game.

1. Collectible Cards: Where to Find Them

Collectible cards are scattered throughout the game world and unlock additional lore about the factions, characters, and history of the world. These cards are often found in hidden locations, requiring you to thoroughly explore every area.

Tips for Collecting Cards:

- **Search Every Building and Vehicle:** Cards can be hidden in the oddest places, such as in abandoned cars, offices, and inside locked chests. Pay attention to areas that you may skip in a hurry.
- **Focus on Hidden Rooms:** Many collectible cards are tucked away in rooms you might miss unless you're looking carefully. Look for hidden access points or small gaps in walls where you can crawl or squeeze through.

- **Track Your Progress:** Use the game's journal or map to keep track of the cards you've collected. You can often find hints about their locations from NPCs or certain collectible item descriptions.

2. Freaker Nests: Clearing Them for Rewards

Throughout *Days Gone Remastered*, Freaker nests serve as an important collectible challenge. Not only do you need to clear all nests to prevent Freakers from spawning, but doing so also unlocks several trophies. These nests are spread across different regions, each containing valuable loot and crafting materials.

Tips for Clearing Nests:

- **Be Stealthy at First:** Before engaging the nest, scout the area and take out any Freakers nearby. Use your crossbow or silenced weapons for stealthy takedowns to avoid alerting the whole area.
- **Use Fire for Maximum Damage:** Molotovs and other incendiary devices are great for clearing nests quickly. Be sure to bring plenty with you.
- **Clear Nests in Stages:** Don't try to clear every nest in one go, especially if you're just starting. Focus on one area at a time and return when you're better equipped.

3. Audio Logs and Diaries: Uncovering the Story

Audio logs and diaries are essential collectibles that provide additional backstory, character development, and insight into the world before the outbreak. These items are scattered across the game world and are essential for completing several trophies.

Tips for Finding Audio Logs:

- **Look in Abandoned Areas:** Audio logs are often found in abandoned vehicles, homes, and structures that are no longer inhabited. Be thorough in your search for these logs in every area you visit.
- **Listen Carefully:** Some logs are hard to spot, so pay attention to areas that have high levels of detail. If you find a suspiciously quiet or eerie location, check for hidden logs.
- **Follow the Story Progression:** Many audio logs are unlocked as you progress through the main story, so be sure to check each area thoroughly as new locations open up.

4. Backpack Locations: Finding Valuable Gear

Backpacks are another type of collectible, and they often contain valuable supplies, crafting materials, and other items that can aid you in your journey. There are numerous backpacks hidden throughout the world of

Days Gone Remastered, and finding them is necessary for completing collectible-related trophies.

Tips for Collecting Backpacks:

- **Check Every Corner:** Backpacks are often tucked away in corners, behind vehicles, or near abandoned structures. Explore every nook and cranny to ensure you don't miss any.

- **Use Your Map:** Mark locations where backpacks are likely to be, such as camps, abandoned vehicles, or areas known for scavenging.

- **Backpacks Are Often Hidden in Plain Sight:** Sometimes backpacks are hanging from trees or stuck under obstacles, so be sure to check unusual locations.

5. Secret Locations and Easter Eggs

Aside from the obvious collectibles, *Days Gone Remastered* has a variety of hidden locations and Easter eggs that reward you for exploring every corner of the game world. These locations may not be required for the main story, but they can add fun and personality to your journey.

Tips for Finding Secret Locations:

- **Look for Unique Landmarks:** Certain locations, such as abandoned diners or old bunkers, may contain hidden collectibles or Easter eggs. Keep an eye out for anything that looks out of place or unique.

- **Interact with Objects:** Some Easter eggs can be triggered by interacting with objects, such as opening specific cabinets or pressing buttons hidden in the environment.

CHAPTER 9: ADVANCED TECHNIQUES

9.1 MASTERING THE MOTORCYCLE: SPEED AND HANDLING TIPS

As you progress through *Days Gone Remastered*, the challenges increase, and you'll need to refine your skills to survive. Whether it's mastering the motorcycle for faster travel or conquering tough boss fights, this chapter delves into the advanced techniques that will elevate your gameplay. From handling the Drifter bike with precision to engaging in strategic combat against the game's most formidable enemies, this guide will provide you with the insights needed to become a true expert.

The motorcycle, or the Drifter bike, is not just a means of transportation in *Days Gone Remastered* it's an essential tool for survival. The open world is vast, and Deacon's bike is crucial for getting from one place to another quickly, dodging Freaker hordes, and making a quick escape when necessary. Mastering the bike's speed, handling, and mechanics can significantly improve your mobility and efficiency, making you a more effective survivor.

1. Understanding the Motorcycle's Mechanics

Before diving into advanced techniques, it's essential to understand the basic mechanics of the Drifter bike. Unlike other vehicles in games, the bike in *Days Gone Remastered* has a unique set of characteristics that affect its speed, stability, and fuel consumption.

Key Components of the Drifter Bike:

- **Throttle and Brakes:** The throttle (R2/RT) and brakes (L2/LT) are your primary tools for controlling speed. The throttle controls acceleration, while the brakes allow you to slow down or stop quickly.

- **Handling and Balance:** The bike's handling is affected by the terrain you drive on. Wet, muddy, or rocky paths will cause the bike to slow down and require more effort to keep balance. Learn to adjust your speed depending on the road conditions.

- **Boost (Circle/B):** The boost feature is an essential tool for outrunning enemies or covering large distances quickly. Use it wisely, as boosting depletes your fuel supply. Always keep an eye on your fuel gauge before engaging the boost.

Basic Tips for Bike Control:

- **Smooth Acceleration:** Avoid sudden, jerky acceleration. Smoothly press the throttle to avoid losing control when riding on uneven terrain. Over-accelerating on rough ground will lead to instability and crashes.

- **Brake Early:** Always brake before entering tight corners or obstacles. Sharp turns or skidding out of control can result in losing precious time or health.

- **Use Boost Strategically:** While the boost helps you cover ground quickly, it's not always the best choice in every scenario. Boosting is ideal for open roads, but on narrower paths or when dodging obstacles, you may want to save your boost for emergencies.

2. Perfecting Cornering and Tight Turns

Handling tight corners and sharp turns is a key skill for mastering the Drifter bike. On high-speed roads, you'll often need to navigate around trees, rocks, or even Freaker hordes, and smooth cornering will help you maintain momentum.

Techniques for Cornering:

- **Lean Into Turns:** When approaching a corner, lean into it by pressing the left analog stick in the direction of the turn. This will help you keep your bike stable, even on difficult terrain.

- **Use the Brake Before Turns:** In situations where you need to slow down for a sharp corner, brake slightly ahead of time and reduce your speed. This will allow you to make the turn smoothly without losing control.

- **Practice in Safe Areas:** When starting out, practice cornering in areas where the threat of enemies is low. This will help you build muscle memory before tackling more dangerous roads or higher speeds.

3. Managing Fuel Consumption

Fuel is an essential resource for your bike, and managing it efficiently is vital for long trips, especially when you're far from safehouses. Relying on your bike's fuel reserves without considering the terrain or distance can leave you stranded in the wilderness with no way to escape.

Tips for Managing Fuel:

- **Refuel Regularly:** Always make it a habit to refuel when you pass a gas station or vehicle. Running out of fuel can leave you vulnerable to Freakers or human factions, so don't wait until you're on empty.

- **Monitor Fuel Efficiency:** When riding through areas with fewer fuel stations, consider adjusting your bike's route to cover more ground with less fuel. Avoid excessive boosting and high speeds to conserve fuel over long distances.

- **Use Fuel Efficiently:** When traveling through heavily populated Freaker zones or areas with heavy terrain, consider reducing speed and saving fuel for emergencies. Boosting too often or driving aggressively will drain your fuel quickly.

4. Escaping Freaker Hordes and Ambushes

Freaker hordes and human ambushes are common threats in *Days Gone Remastered*, and escaping them on your bike is often your best bet. The Drifter bike provides the speed and agility needed to outrun these dangers, but only if you know how to use it effectively.

Escape Tips:

- **Boost to Outrun:** Use your bike's boost to escape a horde or human ambush quickly. Boosting will allow you to put distance between you and the danger, but make sure to have enough fuel in reserve.

- **Use Terrain to Your Advantage:** If you can't outrun enemies on the road, try weaving through trees, rocks, or other natural obstacles. This can slow down the horde or ambushing humans, giving you time to escape.

- **Stay on the Move:** Don't stay in one spot for too long when you're being chased. Constantly change direction to confuse enemies and make it harder for them to predict your path.

9.2 ADVANCED COMBAT: HOW TO TACKLE BOSS FIGHTS

Days Gone Remastered features some intense and challenging boss fights that will test your combat skills, strategy, and resource management. These fights often require you to adapt to different tactics and learn the boss's weaknesses. In this section, we'll guide you through some advanced combat techniques to help you defeat the toughest enemies in the game.

1. Understanding Boss Mechanics

Each boss in *Days Gone Remastered* has its own set of mechanics and weaknesses. Some are more aggressive, while others require specific strategies to defeat. Recognizing these differences is key to successful combat.

Key Boss Fight Tips:

- **Study the Boss Patterns:** Like most games, bosses in *Days Gone* have predictable attack patterns. Spend the first few moments of the fight observing their movements and timing, so you can predict when to dodge or strike.

- **Use Weak Spots:** Many bosses in *Days Gone* have weak spots, such as their heads or specific body parts. Targeting these weak points will deal more damage and help you take down the boss faster.
- **Prepare Your Weapons:** Before engaging in a boss fight, make sure your weapons are fully stocked with ammo and that your bike is fueled. Boss fights can be long and drawn-out, so having enough supplies is crucial.

2. The Importance of Cover and Movement

During boss fights, staying mobile and using cover effectively is crucial. Bosses can deal massive damage with their attacks, so you need to make sure you're always in a safe position to dodge and retaliate.

Cover Strategies:

- **Use the Environment for Protection:** Look for natural cover around you, such as rocks, trees, or abandoned vehicles. These can help protect you from incoming fire and allow you to plan your attacks.
- **Move Constantly:** Standing still during a boss fight makes you an easy target. Keep moving, especially when the boss is charging up a powerful attack. Use your bike or the terrain to move quickly around the area.

3. Exploiting Boss Weaknesses

Most bosses have specific weaknesses that you can exploit to make the fight easier. Whether it's using explosives, targeting weak points, or finding an environmental advantage, knowing how to exploit these weaknesses will give you a significant edge.

Boss Weakness Examples:

- **Fire and Explosives:** Many bosses are weak to fire or explosive damage. Use Molotov cocktails, grenades, or explosive traps to inflict high damage. These can also create area-of-effect damage, allowing you to hit the boss even when you're not directly in its line of sight.
- **Environmental Hazards:** Some bosses can be lured into environmental traps. Use things like explosive barrels, rock formations, or electrical generators to damage or stun the boss. Luring the boss into these traps can turn the tide of battle in your favor.

4. Managing Resources During Boss Fights

Boss fights often require sustained effort and resource management. If you run out of ammo or health kits mid-fight, you'll struggle to win. Efficient use of your resources is essential to surviving and defeating the toughest enemies in *Days Gone Remastered.*

Resource Management Tips:

- **Always Have Health Kits Ready:** Use your health kits at the right time. Don't wait until your health is critically low heal yourself early if you know a big attack is coming.

- **Craft on the Go:** If you run low on ammo, make sure to craft new rounds when possible. Always have your crafting materials ready so you can create Molotovs, pipe bombs, and health kits during the battle.

- **Use All Your Weapons:** Don't rely on just one weapon. Switch between ranged and melee weapons based on the situation. If the boss is far away, use firearms. If they get too close, switch to melee for fast damage.

5. Teaming Up for Boss Fights (Co-Op or Support Missions)

Some of the more challenging boss fights can be tackled more effectively when working with allies or using support tactics. While *Days Gone* is primarily a solo experience, understanding how to use support missions or AI companions will help you defeat particularly tough enemies.

Teamwork Strategies:

- **Use AI Allies:** In certain parts of the game, you'll have the opportunity to team up with AI companions. These allies can help distract the boss, giving you a chance to deal damage from a distance.

- **Co-Op Mode (If Available):** If you're playing in a co-op mode or using a multiplayer feature (if available), team up with friends to tackle difficult bosses. Coordination and teamwork will significantly improve your chances of success.

9.3 EFFICIENT CRAFTING AND RESOURCE GATHERING FOR EXPERTS

In *Days Gone Remastered,* crafting and resource management are key to surviving the harsh wilderness and dealing with the many threats that Deacon faces. Whether you're building essential supplies like health kits, traps, or ammunition, or upgrading your weapons and bike, efficient crafting and resource gathering are crucial. This section will explore expert-level strategies for maximizing your crafting efficiency and gathering the resources needed for success.

1. Crafting the Essentials: Prioritize for Survival

Crafting is a central mechanic in *Days Gone Remastered*. While you can craft a variety of items, some are far more important than others. As an expert player, you'll want to prioritize crafting the items that will keep you alive during tough battles or long journeys.

Essential Crafting Priorities:

- **Health Kits and Stamina Drinks:** These are your most crucial crafting recipes. Always keep enough materials to craft health kits and stamina drinks for extended trips, especially when traversing dangerous zones.
    - o **Tip:** Health kits are especially important when fighting Freaker hordes or during boss fights. Make sure to craft them in advance when you know you'll be facing tough enemies.
- **Molotovs and Pipe Bombs:** These explosives are perfect for taking out large groups of enemies, including Freaker hordes and human factions.
    - o **Tip:** Stockpile Molotov cocktails, especially when you approach horde areas. A well-timed throw can clear out multiple enemies at once and give you breathing room.
- **Trap Crafting:** Craft traps such as proximity mines, bear traps, and flashbangs. These are especially useful in stealth-based encounters or for setting ambushes.
    - o **Tip:** Always have a few traps in your inventory, especially when dealing with larger groups of Freakers or when planning to clear out a Freaker nest.

Efficient Crafting Tips:

- **Use Resource Nodes:** As you explore, look for resource nodes where you can gather materials quickly, such as scrap piles, plants for crafting health kits, and barrels for fuel. Focus on areas rich in these resources.
- **Maximize Resource Use:** Avoid crafting unnecessary items that you won't need. Focus your efforts on the essentials don't waste scrap on crafting low-priority items, like melee weapons, when you should be using it for ammunition or bike upgrades.
- **Craft on the Move:** Use every opportunity to craft on the go, especially during downtime while looting buildings, vehicles, or taking shelter in safe houses. Keep your inventory stocked and ready.

2. Expert Resource Gathering Strategies

Mastering resource gathering is just as important as crafting itself. In *Days Gone Remastered*, the environment is filled with valuable materials, but gathering them efficiently can make the difference between survival and defeat.

Efficient Gathering Tips:

- **Loot Every Structure and Vehicle:** Make it a habit to search every abandoned vehicle, building, and campsite. These locations often contain valuable items like scrap, fuel, ammunition, and crafting components.
  - **Tip:** Abandoned vehicles are particularly useful for fuel, which is vital for your bike. Always stop to siphon fuel when you can.
- **Prioritize High-Value Resources:** While searching the world, prioritize resources that will benefit you the most. Items like scrap, gunpowder, and fuel are often in high demand. Health kit ingredients like plants and alcohol should be collected at every opportunity.
  - **Tip:** When you're near Freaker nests or enemy camps, check the surrounding area for hidden materials. These spots tend to have a high concentration of valuable resources.
- **Use the Map to Track Resource Locations:** Use your in-game map to mark locations where you've found a high concentration of resources. This helps streamline your search and ensures that you don't miss key spots when you need them the most.
- **Check Resource-Rich Locations First:** Areas like gas stations, abandoned military outposts, and survivor camps usually have the highest resource yields. Make these places your first stop when you're gathering supplies.

Advanced Resource Tips:

- **Keep Inventory Full:** Always ensure that your inventory is as full as possible, especially when preparing for large missions or dangerous areas. This ensures you're prepared for any combat situation and will minimize the risk of running out of supplies.
- **Don't Overload:** Be mindful of your inventory space, especially for bulky items like fuel or crafting materials. Don't gather more than you can carry unless you plan to drop items or store them at a safehouse.

3. Upgrading Your Gear Efficiently

Upgrading your weapons, bike, and gear is essential for tackling tougher challenges in the game. Efficient upgrades allow you to carry more supplies, deal more damage, and survive longer in the wild. Prioritize upgrading your gear based on your playing style.

Weapon Upgrades:

- **Focus on Ranged Weapons:** Upgrading your firearms (rifles, shotguns, crossbows) is crucial for dealing with large groups of enemies or tougher adversaries. Focus on increasing ammo capacity, damage, and reload speed to maximize your combat effectiveness.

- **Maximize the Utility of Melee Weapons:** Melee weapons are often a more resource-efficient option for handling smaller groups of Freakers. Consider upgrading your melee weapons to extend their durability and increase damage output.

Bike Upgrades:

- **Fuel Tank and Storage:** One of the most important bike upgrades is the fuel tank, as this increases the range of your bike and reduces the frequency of needing to refuel. Upgrading the storage capacity will help you carry more supplies, making your trips more efficient.

- **Performance Mods:** Invest in upgrades for speed, handling, and durability. These will allow you to escape more quickly from dangerous situations or outpace Freaker hordes on your bike.

9.4 SPEEDRUNNING TECHNIQUES FOR *Days Gone Remastered*

For players who are looking for an added challenge or simply want to finish *Days Gone Remastered* as quickly as possible, speedrunning is an exciting way to experience the game. Speedrunning is about completing the game in the shortest time possible, often using advanced techniques to skip sections, exploit glitches, or optimize your route.

While *Days Gone* is a large, open-world game that may seem ill-suited for speedrunning, it's possible to complete it in record time with the right strategies. This section will provide you with techniques to help you speed through *Days Gone Remastered* as quickly as possible.

1. Route Optimization: Skip Unnecessary Side Objectives

In speedrunning, the key is to minimize your travel time and avoid unnecessary detours. Focusing only on the core missions and skipping side objectives will allow you to progress more quickly.

Tips for Route Optimization:

- **Stick to Main Story Missions:** In a typical speedrun, you'll want to focus only on the main story missions. This means avoiding side activities like clearing out Freaker nests, completing challenges, or gathering collectibles.
- **Use Fast Travel Wisely:** Fast travel can cut down on travel time significantly, but be mindful of its limitations. Fast travel is only available once you've unlocked certain areas, so you'll need to plan ahead to make sure you're not wasting time.
- **Plan Efficient Travel Routes:** Use your bike to move quickly between mission objectives, and always keep an eye on the map for shorter routes that avoid large enemy encampments or horde zones.

2. Mastering Combat for Speed

Combat can be a major time sink in *Days Gone Remastered*, but there are ways to make it faster and more efficient. Speedrunning requires a keen understanding of when to fight and when to avoid enemies altogether.

Combat Efficiency Tips:

- **Avoid Unnecessary Fights:** Don't engage with every enemy you encounter. Focus on clearing the path to your next objective without wasting time on unnecessary skirmishes. Use stealth or simply outrun enemies when possible.
- **Use High-Damage, Low Ammo Weapons:** Opt for weapons that deal massive damage but require fewer shots to eliminate enemies. The **rifle** and **shotgun** are excellent choices for taking out multiple enemies with minimal effort.
- **Exploit Weak Points:** Target enemy weak points to end fights faster. Headshots on both Freakers and humans can significantly reduce the number of hits required to defeat them.

3. Use of Boosting and Avoiding Slowdowns

Boosting on your bike is one of the most effective ways to save time in a speedrun. However, you need to manage your fuel and use boosting strategically to avoid running out at crucial moments.

Boosting Tips:

- **Conserve Fuel for Boosting:** Only use your boost when necessary to maintain speed. Running out of fuel can slow down your progress, so keep an eye on your bike's fuel level and stop at gas stations when possible.

- **Take Advantage of Boost in Open Areas:** Boosting is most effective in open areas, where there are few obstacles. Use it when traveling across large stretches of land to speed up your journey.
- **Use Your Bike to Skip Obstacles:** Boosting can help you avoid or quickly pass over obstacles, such as rocks or fallen trees. Mastering this can make your routes much faster and more efficient.

4. Exploiting Game Glitches and Shortcuts

Some speedrunners exploit game glitches and shortcuts to cut down on time. While not always intentional, these techniques can provide significant time savings if you know where and how to use them.

Glitch and Shortcut Tips:

- **Skip Animations and Cutscenes:** Some speedruns involve skipping lengthy animations or cutscenes that are non-essential. Mastering the timing of skipping these sections can save you valuable seconds or even minutes.
- **Map Glitches or Unintended Shortcuts:** Certain areas of the map may be easier to access through unintended routes or glitches. Learning these shortcuts can help you shave minutes off your time.
- **Study Other Speedruns:** Watch videos from other experienced speedrunners to see how they utilize glitches and shortcuts. Their routes and techniques can offer valuable insight into how you can improve your own run.

CHAPTER 10: ADDITIONAL RESOURCES

10.1 COMMUNITY TIPS AND STRATEGIES

In this final chapter, we'll dive into the additional resources that can enhance your experience in *Days Gone Remastered*. Whether you're looking for tips and strategies from the community or analyzing the deeper layers of the game's story through fan theories and breakdowns, this chapter will help you connect with the broader *Days Gone* experience. There's much more to this game than what's covered in the guide, and the *Days Gone* community and the game's rich lore offer plenty of fascinating discussions and insights.

The *Days Gone* community is full of passionate players who have spent countless hours perfecting their gameplay. Whether it's finding new ways to survive, improving your combat skills, or uncovering hidden secrets, the community is a goldmine of helpful tips and strategies that can improve your overall experience.

1. Exploring the *Days Gone* Forums and Subreddits

The first place to turn for expert advice and tips is online forums and subreddits. The *Days Gone* subreddit and dedicated gaming forums are filled with seasoned players who are always willing to share their knowledge. Here, you can find discussions on strategies, guides, and even specific threads dedicated to uncovering all the game's secrets.

What You'll Find:

- **Strategy Guides:** Many players share detailed guides on how to complete specific missions or take down difficult bosses.
- **Resource Locations:** Community members post maps and resources showing the locations of important items like Nero injectors, weapon upgrades, and Freaker nest locations.
- **Gameplay Techniques:** You'll discover advanced techniques, such as exploiting the game's mechanics for faster travel, getting more resources, and maximizing your chances of survival in tough encounters.

Recommended Resources:

- **r/DaysGone on Reddit:** A lively community where players share their experiences, tips, and theories.
- **Days Gone Wiki:** A comprehensive source for information on every aspect of the game, from missions to collectibles.

2. YouTube and Twitch: Watch and Learn

For players who learn best visually, YouTube and Twitch provide fantastic platforms for watching skilled gamers and content creators in action. Watching *Days Gone* gameplay streams and videos can teach you valuable strategies and give you insight into how experts approach the game.

What You'll Learn:

- **Speedrunning:** There are dedicated *Days Gone* speedrunners on YouTube and Twitch who share their runs and strategies. This can help you perfect your own speedrun techniques.
- **Combat Tips:** Many streamers focus on high-level combat techniques, showcasing how to take on large hordes, engage in boss fights, and manage resources during difficult scenarios.
- **Exploration and Collectibles:** Watch walkthroughs to find all the collectibles and hidden items, as well as how to approach tricky exploration challenges.

Recommended Channels:

- **YouTube Guides:** Search for channels dedicated to *Days Gone* walkthroughs, tips, and speedrunning.
- **Twitch Streams:** Live streamers provide real-time, interactive gameplay, allowing you to ask questions and learn strategies as you watch.

3. Joining Online Communities for Co-op Play and Multiplayer

While *Days Gone* is primarily a single-player game, many fans enjoy playing with others in multiplayer games or cooperative settings. Joining a gaming community gives you the chance to connect with other players, discuss strategies, and even join co-op events or multiplayer challenges.

What You'll Find:

- **Multiplayer Challenges:** Participate in community-hosted challenges where players can compete or cooperate to complete difficult objectives.
- **Co-op Strategies:** Some players develop co-op strategies for tackling harder missions or surviving longer in the world of *Days Gone*.

How to Get Involved:

- **Discord Servers:** Many *Days Gone* players connect through Discord, where you can chat with others, find co-op partners, or engage in discussions about the game.
- **Co-op Events:** Keep an eye out for events where players come together to challenge large hordes or bosses in multiplayer mode.

10.2 FAN THEORIES AND STORY BREAKDOWN

The narrative of *Days Gone Remastered* is deep, complex, and open to interpretation. With its emotional moments, ambiguous characters, and mysterious backstory, the game has sparked a variety of fan theories and discussions about its story and universe. This section will explore some of the most popular fan theories and provide a breakdown of the game's lore and narrative to give you a deeper understanding of the world.

1. The Connection Between Deacon and the Freaker Virus

One of the most discussed fan theories revolves around the possible connection between Deacon's resilience to the Freaker virus and his immunity. Throughout the game, Deacon seems to show a remarkable ability to resist infection and maintain his humanity despite his exposure to the virus, which raises questions about whether he has a unique immunity or if there's another reason he hasn't succumbed to the virus like most others.

Theories:

- **Deacon's Immunity:** Some fans speculate that Deacon may have a special resistance to the virus due to his background, possibly connected to his past as a soldier or the influence of the Nero research program. This theory suggests that Deacon's immunity could play a pivotal role in finding a cure or understanding the virus's full potential.

- **Deacon as an Experiment:** Another popular theory suggests that Deacon was unknowingly part of an experiment by the Nero organization, which might explain his resistance to the virus.

Supporting Evidence:

- **Nero Injectors:** The discovery of Nero injectors in the game raises the possibility that Deacon may have been exposed to these experimental treatments.

- **Survival Against All Odds:** Deacon's ability to endure the virus and survive in a world filled with infected individuals who don't have the same strength points to a larger mystery surrounding his immune system.

2. Sarah's Fate and the Connection to the Freakers

Sarah's disappearance is a key plot point in *Days Gone Remastered*. While the game strongly hints that she was lost to the Freaker outbreak, some fans believe there might be more to her story.

Theories:

- **Sarah's Survival:** Some fans speculate that Sarah might have been turned into a Freaker or experimented on by Nero, and that she could potentially play a pivotal role in the game's future storyline or sequel.
- **Sarah's Role in the Cure:** Another theory revolves around Sarah's connection to the research conducted by Nero. Many believe that her involvement in the virus research might make her central to discovering a cure or unraveling the truth behind the outbreak.

Supporting Evidence:
- **Sarah's Background in Research:** Sarah's medical background and her ties to Nero suggest she might have had a deeper understanding of the Freaker virus, potentially leading to a discovery that could save humanity.
- **Hints from Deacon's Memories:** Throughout the game, Deacon has flashbacks of Sarah, hinting at her possible involvement in the greater narrative and suggesting that her story is far from over.

3. The Rippers and Their True Motive

The Rippers are one of the most disturbing and enigmatic factions in *Days Gone Remastered*. Led by the charismatic and psychotic leader, Schizo, the Rippers believe in the power of the Freaker virus, considering themselves superior to other survivors. But what exactly is their true motive?

Theories:
- **The Rippers as a Cult:** Many fans believe that the Rippers are not just a faction, but a cult, worshipping the Freakers and seeing themselves as the "next evolution" of humanity. This theory suggests that their actions are part of a twisted religious belief that the Freaker virus is the key to transcendence.
- **Rippers as Experiment Subjects:** Another theory suggests that the Rippers were part of a failed experiment by the Nero organization. They may have been exposed to a more aggressive strain of the virus, which drove them to insanity and caused their belief in the Freakers as a higher form of life.

Supporting Evidence:
- **Ripper Behavior and Rituals:** The Rippers' actions and rituals suggest that they view the Freakers as a higher power. Their brutal treatment of survivors and obsession with the virus further supports the idea of a twisted religious or experimental agenda.
- **Schizo's Leadership:** Schizo's character is central to the Rippers' influence, and his backstory might reveal more about their origins and ultimate goals.

4. The Future of *Days Gone* and the Sequel

As with many open-world games, fans are eager to speculate about the future of *Days Gone*. With the game's immense world-building, complex characters, and open-ended storyline, there's plenty to explore in a potential sequel.

Theories:

- **The Search for a Cure:** Fans believe that a sequel could focus on Deacon's journey to find a cure for the Freaker virus, potentially involving Sarah's research or a deeper dive into the Nero organization's experiments.

- **New Enemies and Factions:** A sequel could introduce new, even more dangerous factions, such as other survivor groups that have evolved differently than Deacon's, or mutated Freakers that have adapted to the world over time.

- **The Role of the Motorcycle:** The Drifter bike is integral to *Days Gone*, and many theorists believe that a sequel could introduce more customization options, new types of vehicles, or even a larger emphasis on bike-based gameplay.

Supporting Evidence:

- **Endgame Hints:** The final chapters of *Days Gone Remastered* leave plenty of questions unanswered, such as the fate of the Freakers and the future of the survivors.

- **Community Speculation:** The community is already rife with ideas about the future of the series, including new locations to explore, new characters to meet, and greater challenges to face.

10.3 UPDATES AND DLC CONTENT FOR *Days Gone Remastered*

Since its release, *Days Gone Remastered* has seen a series of updates and downloadable content (DLC) that add exciting new features, challenges, and narrative elements to the game. Whether you're looking for fresh storylines, tougher enemies, or additional gameplay mechanics, the updates and DLC packs provide an expanded experience that enhances the core game. This section breaks down the major updates and DLC content released for *Days Gone Remastered* and how they can enrich your gameplay.

1. Key DLC Packs for *Days Gone Remastered*

Several DLC packs were released post-launch to provide new story content, survival challenges, and cosmetic upgrades. These packs offer a deeper dive into the *Days Gone* universe and give players more to explore.

DLC Packs:

- **Survival Mode DLC:** This DLC introduces an even more punishing version of the game where resources are more limited, enemies are tougher, and the world feels even more desolate. Survival Mode is perfect for players looking for a hardcore challenge and additional replay value.
    - o **What to Expect:** Increased difficulty, less ammo, tougher enemies, and the need for more strategic planning. Completing Survival Mode unlocks additional achievements and rewards.
- **Challenges Mode DLC:** Challenge Mode offers various gameplay challenges, such as horde battles, time trials, and resource scavenger hunts. Each challenge is designed to test your skills, speed, and efficiency.
    - o **What to Expect:** New maps and environments to complete specific goals, such as clearing a specific number of Freakers within a time limit. Successfully completing these challenges will unlock unique gear and rewards, including special skins for weapons and the bike.
- **The "Trust" DLC:** The "Trust" DLC offers deeper faction-based gameplay, allowing you to work closely with different survivor camps. This DLC lets you earn trust more quickly with factions, unlocking new storylines, side missions, and exclusive gear.
    - o **What to Expect:** A focus on faction dynamics and deeper relationships with NPCs, offering more narrative content and additional missions tied to faction progression.

2. Major Game Updates

Alongside DLC releases, *Days Gone Remastered* has seen multiple updates that improve gameplay balance, fix bugs, and introduce quality-of-life improvements.

Major Updates:

- **Performance Enhancements:** The Remastered version has been optimized for modern consoles, with improvements in graphical fidelity, frame rates, and overall performance. These updates ensure that the game runs smoothly on all supported hardware.
- **New Difficulty Options:** Updates have included the addition of new difficulty settings for players who want an even more challenging experience. These settings modify the frequency of enemy spawns, the damage dealt by enemies, and the availability of resources.

- **Bug Fixes and Quality-of-Life Improvements:** Players have received various updates addressing bugs and glitches, improving the overall stability of the game. These updates also included minor tweaks to gameplay mechanics and user interface improvements, making the game more enjoyable.

3. How to Access DLC and Updates

To enjoy the latest content, make sure your game is up to date with all the latest patches and DLCs. Here's how to access these features:

- **Automatic Updates:** For console players, *Days Gone Remastered* automatically downloads updates and patches once your system is connected to the internet. Ensure that automatic updates are enabled in your system settings.
- **Purchasing DLC:** To access additional downloadable content, head to your platform's digital store (PlayStation Store, Steam, etc.). Some DLC packs are free, while others may need to be purchased separately.
- **Check for New Content Regularly:** Developers often release new updates or time-limited DLCs, so check the game's official website, your platform's store, or community forums to stay updated on the latest content.

10.4 MODDING AND CUSTOMIZATION RESOURCES

While *Days Gone Remastered* is not known for a heavily modded community, modding and customization still offer an exciting way for players to alter their experience. Customization in *Days Gone* extends beyond just your gear and weapons, as modding allows players to tweak gameplay elements, enhance visuals, and introduce new challenges or features. In this section, we'll cover the available resources for modding *Days Gone Remastered* and provide tips on how to customize your experience.

1. Overview of Modding for *Days Gone Remastered*

Days Gone Remastered was designed with a relatively open-world structure, making it more conducive to modding compared to linear games. While mods are not officially supported by the developers, the modding community has found creative ways to enhance the game. Modding typically focuses on visual improvements, gameplay tweaks, and new challenges.

Common Types of Mods:

- **Visual Mods:** Mods that enhance the graphics, including texture improvements, lighting changes, and environmental tweaks. These mods may improve the realism of the game or offer a different aesthetic.

- **Gameplay Mods:** Mods that change how the game plays, such as adjusting difficulty, modifying AI behavior, or tweaking the behavior of enemies and NPCs. Some mods offer increased difficulty or provide new challenges that go beyond the official DLC content.
- **Bike Customization Mods:** Mods focused on the Drifter bike, allowing players to unlock custom skins, change the appearance of the bike, or even modify its performance.
- **Sound Mods:** Changes to the game's audio, such as custom music tracks or altered environmental sounds, can immerse you in a different experience.
- **Cheat Mods:** While not ideal for all players, some mods allow for cheats, like infinite health or resources, which may appeal to those looking for a more relaxed or creative playthrough.

2. How to Install Mods on PC

If you're playing *Days Gone Remastered* on PC, installing mods can be straightforward. However, it's important to note that modding carries some risk, including potential crashes or other issues if not done correctly. Always back up your game data before installing mods to prevent loss of progress.

Step-by-Step Modding Process:

1. **Find Reliable Modding Sources:** Websites like Nexus Mods and Mod DB are great places to find mods for *Days Gone Remastered*. These sites offer a variety of mods, including graphics enhancements, gameplay tweaks, and more.
2. **Download the Mod:** Once you find a mod you like, download it from a trusted source. Ensure that the mod is compatible with your game version.
3. **Install the Mod:** Some mods come with an installer, while others need to be manually placed into the game's directory. Read the mod description carefully for installation instructions.
4. **Backup Your Files:** Before installing mods, always back up your game's files, especially if you're replacing core files. This will allow you to revert to the original game version if needed.
5. **Test the Mod:** After installation, launch the game and check whether the mod works as expected. If the game crashes or there are issues, consult the mod's community or the mod creator for troubleshooting tips.

Important Modding Tips:

- **Stay Updated:** Mods can break after game updates, so make sure to check for updates or new versions of the mod after each game patch.

- **Read Reviews:** Before installing mods, read reviews and feedback from other players to ensure the mod is stable and works as intended.
- **Compatibility:** Some mods may conflict with others. Avoid installing too many mods at once and test them one by one to ensure they function correctly.

3. Customizing Your Bike and Gear

Customization plays a big role in *Days Gone Remastered*, allowing players to alter the appearance of their gear, weapons, and bike. While the official game offers limited options for customization, mods can unlock even more options and make your gear truly unique.

Customization Options:

- **Bike Skins and Paint Jobs:** Many modders offer custom skins and paint jobs for the Drifter bike, allowing you to personalize its appearance.
- **Weapon Skins:** Mods can add different skins for weapons, including guns and melee weapons, to help them stand out or reflect a certain theme.
- **Outfit Mods for Deacon:** Modders may create unique outfits for Deacon, altering his appearance and adding flair to the character model.

Installing Customizations:

- **Manual Installation:** Some customization mods require you to manually install them into the game's files, similar to how you would install other mods.
- **Tools for Customization:** Some advanced mods come with their own tools or modding interfaces to help you create or tweak custom assets without needing to modify the game files directly.

4. Participating in the Modding Community

For players who want to dive deeper into modding, the modding community around *Days Gone Remastered* provides a wealth of information. From guides to tutorials, joining modding communities can help you learn more about modding and even contribute your own creations.

Popular Modding Communities:

- **Nexus Mods Forum:** A huge community dedicated to modding various games, including *Days Gone Remastered*. Here you can ask questions, share your mods, or get advice on installation.

- **Discord Servers:** Many modders operate within dedicated Discord servers, where they collaborate, discuss, and troubleshoot mods together.
- **YouTube and Tutorials:** For visual learners, YouTube hosts a variety of modding tutorials that show how to install mods, create new content, and customize *Days Gone Remastered* to your liking.

CHAPTER 11: FINAL THOUGHTS AND EXTRA INSIGHTS

11.1 FINAL THOUGHTS AND RECOMMENDATIONS

As we wrap up this comprehensive guide to *Days Gone Remastered*, it's important to reflect on the game's journey, the strategies shared, and the overall experience that awaits you in this vast, post-apocalyptic world. This chapter will offer final thoughts and recommendations for both newcomers and veteran players, as well as acknowledge those who helped bring this guide to life.

Days Gone Remastered is a game that thrives on its open world, engaging mechanics, and emotional storytelling. Whether you're navigating the treacherous roads on your bike, clearing out horde zones, or delving into the deeper narrative about survival and loss, the game offers something for everyone.

1. A Story with Emotional Depth

At its core, *Days Gone* is about Deacon's struggle to survive in a world overrun by the infected and where trust among humans is scarce. The game's emotional depth is one of its strongest attributes, particularly in Deacon's relationships with his wife, Sarah, and his companions. The storyline is crafted to pull at the heartstrings while keeping you on edge with unpredictable moments and action sequences.

Recommendation:

- Take your time to immerse yourself in the narrative. Don't rush through the story just to reach the end. The side missions and interactions with other survivors add emotional weight to the story and can offer more personal reflections on Deacon's journey.

2. Combat and Strategy are Key

The game's combat mechanics are diverse and challenging, especially in the more difficult settings. Whether it's taking down Freakers with a variety of weapons or engaging in firefights with hostile factions, the game provides ample opportunities to refine your combat skills. Learning when to fight and when to avoid conflict is just as crucial as mastering the technical aspects of the gameplay.

Recommendation:

- Experiment with different weapons and tactics. Stealth isn't always the best approach, especially when facing large hordes. Mix your combat strategies by using explosives, traps, and your bike to escape dangerous situations.

3. Explore Every Corner of the World

The world of *Days Gone Remastered* is vast and filled with secrets. There are countless collectibles, hidden resources, and challenges that reward curiosity. It's not just about completing missions taking the time to explore will reward you with valuable materials, powerful weapons, and lore that enriches the game's universe.

Recommendation:

- Don't hesitate to explore the backroads, abandoned camps, and remote areas. Many of the game's best rewards are hidden away in places you might not initially notice. Be thorough and prepared for anything.

4. Prepare for Long-Term Survival

In *Days Gone Remastered*, survival isn't just about defeating enemies. It's about managing your resources, upgrading your gear, and making careful decisions that ensure your survival in the long term. Always be aware of your inventory and fuel levels, and plan ahead when heading into dangerous areas.

Recommendation:

- Regularly upgrade your bike and weapons, and focus on crafting supplies like health kits and explosives. Efficient resource gathering and smart crafting choices are crucial to staying ahead of the game's increasing difficulty.

5. Play at Your Own Pace

One of the game's greatest strengths is its ability to cater to different playstyles. Whether you want to rush through the main story, engage in every side mission, or explore the world at your leisure, *Days Gone Remastered* offers flexibility. You're free to experience the game on your terms, and the rewards for doing so are plenty.

Recommendation:

- Play at your own pace. While it's tempting to rush through the main plot, take your time to explore side quests and personal storylines. The depth and richness of the world will make the experience more fulfilling.

11.2 ACKNOWLEDGMENTS AND CREDITS

Creating a comprehensive guide to *Days Gone Remastered* is a team effort, and I would like to express my gratitude to all those who contributed to this project. From the developers of the game to the passionate community of players, every bit of effort has helped shape this experience into something special.

1. Acknowledging the Developers

A big thank you goes to the talented team at Bend Studio, the creators of *Days Gone*. Their hard work and attention to detail have resulted in a game that captivates players with its dynamic world, emotionally charged narrative, and engaging gameplay mechanics. *Days Gone Remastered* is a testament to the creativity and dedication of the team who crafted the world of Deacon St. John.

Special Mentions:

- **John Garvin:** Game Director and Writer, whose storytelling and vision brought the world of *Days Gone* to life.
- **Jeff Ross:** Game Director, whose contributions to the game's mechanics and open-world design shaped the game's immersive experience.
- **Bend Studio Team:** The programmers, artists, designers, and sound engineers who worked tirelessly to create the game's stunning visuals, dynamic world, and immersive soundscapes.

2. Thanking the Community

The *Days Gone* community has been an invaluable resource for this guide. Through fan theories, strategy tips, and a wealth of experience shared on forums and social media platforms, the community continues to expand the understanding of *Days Gone Remastered*. Many of the tips, theories, and strategies found in this guide come directly from these dedicated fans.

Special Mentions:

- **Reddit /r/DaysGone:** The active subreddit where fans engage in discussions, share insights, and provide support to newcomers.
- **Nexus Mods and Other Modding Communities:** For contributing to the customization and modding resources that offer players fresh and exciting ways to experience the game.
- **YouTube Streamers and Content Creators:** Whose walkthroughs and tips helped players tackle difficult missions and uncover hidden secrets in the game.

3. A Personal Thank You

Lastly, I'd like to extend a heartfelt thank you to all the readers who have taken the time to explore this guide. Whether you're a new player or a seasoned veteran of *Days Gone*, your dedication to understanding every detail of the game and improving your gameplay is truly inspiring. I hope that this guide has provided you with the knowledge and confidence to master the game, uncover all its secrets, and enjoy the story of Deacon St. John to its fullest.